Who's Got *You*?

*Observations of a
Catholic Homeschooling Father*

by John Clark

Who's Got *You*?

Observations of a Catholic Homeschooling Father

by John Clark

Copyright © 2012 Seton Home Study School
All rights reserved. No part of this book may be reproduced without written permission of the publisher, except by a reviewer who may quote brief passages in a review.
Printed in the United States of America.
ISBN: 978-1-60704-096-5
Published by Seton Press.
Visit us on the Web at http://www.setonbooks.com/

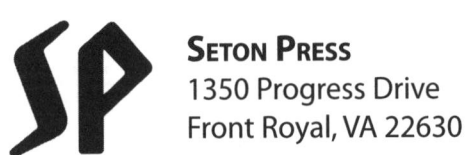

SETON PRESS
1350 Progress Drive
Front Royal, VA 22630

This book is affectionately dedicated to St. Joseph.

Contents

Acknowledgements . . . . *vii*
Introduction . . . . *ix*

Section 1: Prayers

Who's Got You? 1
What's at Stake 5
The Father's Role 10
The Sound 14
The Mercy of Fatherhood 19
Back in the Box 22
Hello, Good Men 26
A Love Letter 30
Before the Throne of God 34

Section 2: Works

Higher Learning 39
Home (Schooling) Economics 44
A New Year 48
Unknown Subjects 52
Time and Tide 56
It's a Wonderful Life 59
Energetic Reading 62
Checks and Balances 65
Lost in Translation 69

Section 3: Sufferings

Fish Stories *73*
On Sleep *76*
64 Degrees of Separation *80*
Decaf *83*
Long Division *87*
Fifty *91*
No Rest for the Weary *95*
Television and Lent *98*
Mere Fatherhood *102*

Section 4: Joys

Eight Isn't Enough *108*
Forty *112*
Love Story *118*
A Night Out *121*
Under the Sea…Almost *124*
Raspberry Sorbet *128*
Conversations with Children *134*
Plum Pudding and Scrabble *138*

Afterword: Questions, Answers, and Errors *143*
Works Cited *146*

Acknowledgements

No one ever writes a book alone. Though that's true for all books, it's especially true for this one. First of all, I should thank my brother, Ken Clark, who encouraged me to put my thoughts into book form.

I have been blessed with excellent editors and assistants, including Mary Kay Clark, Jane Elliot, Rob Jones, Joe Sparks, Lisa Marciano, Kevin Clark, Sarah Daley, Kathryn Kujawski, Emily Sparks, Christine Smitha, and Stephen Phelan. Thank you for making this book better.

Of course, this book is a journal of my life and those I love. I could not have done any of this without my wife, Lisa, or my children, whom you are about to come to know.

Thanks for reading.

Introduction

Many Catholic families start their day with a prayer called the Morning Offering. It begins: "O Jesus, through the Immaculate Heart of Mary, I offer Thee all my prayers, works, sufferings, and joys of this day…"

The Morning Offering is a prayer of worship, but it is also a prayer of friendship. What you're asking in this prayer is very simple. You're saying, "Whatever happens today, whether good or bad, please be with me—please stay by my side, because I love You, and I believe You love me." But it alludes to another truth: that we *will* have prayers, works, sufferings, and joys, and how we react to these determines much of who we are.

In these pages, I have let you peek in on my family's life—on the prayers, works, sufferings, and joys of the Clark family. Although these stories are about us, my guess is that they are, in a sense, about *your* family, too. I have received many compliments about my articles in the past few years, and I am very grateful for these compliments. But I think that the source of joy for other people in reading these essays is that they see their own families in the printed word. In their letters, I think what people were saying more than anything was, "my family is like that, too." The most important things—the things that endure—are common to many Catholic families.

My hope is that these essays help fathers understand more fully why they should appreciate their lives. To put it more simply, I have tried to show fathers why they should be laughing instead of crying.

It is with deep affection that I approach good and strong fathers. The responsibilities of fatherhood can be overwhelming. They can make us tremble. But what if no one accepted the challenge of fatherhood?

I've wondered what it would be like if, instead of growing up on earth and becoming a father naturally, fathers were recruited from a batch of men in Limbo. An angel might appear to them, tell them that there was a job needed on earth, and ask men for volunteers. The angel might then explain the job in the following way:

"You will be responsible for little boys and girls. In the first few years, they will not be able to do much of anything for themselves. You will need to feed them and clothe them and protect them. You will need to nurture them. When they suffer, you will feel their pain more than they do. You will need to teach them about God, while many others on earth will lie to them and tell them that God does not exist. You must pray very hard for them, because they will be tempted to turn away from everything you love and believe most. They will be tempted to turn away from you, and believe that they no longer need you. They will be tempted to think that you don't understand them, even though you may understand more than anyone else. They will be tempted to think you don't love them as much as others, even though you love them more than anyone else. In the end, if you're called to do so, you must be willing to lay down your life for them."

When asked, a man might say: "Why would I want *that*?"

Then the angel might respond:

"Because God loves *you*.

"Because the first time you feel the baby kick in your wife's belly, *you* will love what you cannot yet see.

"Because God wants *you* to understand more fully what love is.

"Because God believes in *you*.

"Because God is willing to entrust *you* with His most precious gift.

"Because there may be no better way for *you* to love God than to love as a father."

Fatherhood is a tremendous responsibility. The modern world understands that, which is why few want the responsibility, and even fewer see it through. What is less understood is that fatherhood is a blessing of incomprehensible magnitude. While other men run away from responsibility, we Catholic fathers need to embrace it.

Section 1: Prayers

Who's Got *You*?

During a blizzard that dumped about three feet of snow on the little hamlet of Front Royal, Virginia, our house lost electric power for hours at a time. The children excitedly hunted down the emergency flashlights and prepared for nighttime with their trusted, illuminating friends. As dusk waned, however, the novelty of the flashlights wore off as it dawned on the children that they would be sleeping in the dark. Ten minutes after Lisa and I put the children to bed, my little two-year-old daughter, Immaculata, called me from her bedroom, and whimpered, "Daddy, I'm scared." I went into her room, gave her a hug, and assured her that I would protect her, reminding her: "I'm with you, Immaculata. I'm watching over you. Nothing bad will happen to you tonight."

Whatever bogeymen haunted her thoughts were no match for her Daddy. The nighttime world of shadows and gloomy uncertainty was overcome by the knowledge that her Daddy was in the next room, ready to dispel any unwelcome visitors, seen or unseen. As I relate this story, keep in mind, I have no delusions of grandeur. I have no special powers of defense beyond that of mortal man. I have no heroic ability. I have one qualification that made Immaculata feel safe, and only one: I am her Daddy, but that's a pretty big deal. I was once in her shoes (or slippers, as the case may be). I still remember dozing off to sleep as a little boy, hearing my dad in the next room, whether talking to my mom, doing some carpentry, or playing cards with my brothers. Whatever my dad was doing, he was there in the house; and with him there, nothing bad would happen to me.

What I *didn't* realize as a little boy, and what most little children don't realize, is that their daddies have times when *they* feel scared, too. Some bogeymen are real. They may not lurk in closets or under the bed, but they manifest themselves in other ways, like when their children are sick, when their jobs are insecure, or when the homeschooling falls behind. Sometimes the financial monsters seem so big against little paychecks. Sometimes the bogeyman whispers to daddies to give up: that they can't do it all anymore. Yes, daddies get scared, too. And yet, we fathers have to be the rocks of stability. We're expected to be superheroes at times when just being mild-mannered men seems a struggle.

In the 1977 movie version of *Superman*, there is a scene in which damsel-in-distress Lois Lane falls helplessly off a tall building to her seemingly certain death. As she screams in terror, Clark Kent quickly changes into Superman garb, flies up to Lois, holds her and says, "Don't worry, I've got you!" Lois responds with a very natural question, crying out: "You've got me? Who's got *you*?" Superman responds with a look of supreme confidence that seems to say to her: "I know you're worried, but the truth is you've never been safer in your life."

Immaculata never asked Lois' question, but she would have every right to ask, "Who's got *you*?" With all the troubles we fathers have in this life, in this vale of tears, why don't children ask, "Who's got *you*?"

Maybe it is because they already know, or at least *sense* the answer, because there *is* an answer to the question. The reason that we can look in our children's worried eyes and answer with confidence just as Superman did is because we fathers know the answer too.

"Who's got *me?*"

"*God* has me."

That is the *secret* of our strength; that is the *source* of our strength: God has me.

Of course, there are ways that we can get closer to Him. None of us fathers seem to have much time, but we can all incorporate three things that take about fifteen minutes each that will bring us much closer to Jesus: Confession, Adoration, and the Rosary.

Sin pushes God away, but sacramental Confession brings Him closer to us. In one glorious moment, a lifetime of sin can be absolved, and God is always close to a repentant heart. Make monthly Confession a habit, and you'll discover that peace becomes a habit.

Take a few minutes each day, or at least a few times a week, to kneel before the Blessed Sacrament and tell Jesus your troubles. Sanctifying grace makes us friends with Jesus, and this friendship was purchased by Him at a great price. Time spent talking with Jesus in Adoration is quality time.

Spend time in the Rosary asking Mary to help you glorify her Divine Son. Leading the family Rosary is a reminder to the children where your strength *really* comes from.

In these times of war, financial hardship, and other forms of uncertainty, life's been coming at us pretty fast. But instead of letting things overwhelm us, let's pray for the grace to "walk by faith, not by sight." Let's take a few minutes to think about all those times that worried us before, and yet, God was with us, and He helped us overcome them. Those difficulties were no match for a loving God, and neither are the difficulties we have now. Jesus is holding us faithful Christians to His Sacred Heart, and gently whispering to us, "I know you're worried, but you've never been safer than you are right now."

What's at Stake

Considering that I have the worst directional sense of anyone I know, I recently bought a global positioning satellite (GPS) instrument for my car. Now I never get lost driving because I always know where I am. I can even "see" myself progressing up the road, and always be assured that I am on the right track. My destination is even marked with a little checkered flag, and I can track my car moving right towards it.

Here's the problem with the GPS: it doesn't work for other areas of my life, like homeschooling. For instance, I can't open the Seton History 8 book and see my children following a direct route to Heaven as they read it. Maybe life for homeschooling families would be easier if we *could* see this progression. It might be easier, but perhaps that's where faith comes in.

Because we can't visually track our movement and our children's advances, and because at times we lack faith, homeschooling can sometimes seem too heavy a burden to carry. If you're going through a period like this, let me offer you a piece of advice: remember why you made this decision. Remember your mission.

Because in the course of homeschooling, if you forget why you began, it's all over but the shouting.

It is said that when married couples are experiencing tough times, they should try to remember why they fell in love. We fathers often must remind ourselves why we homeschool in the first place.

Though we fathers may have had similar reasons for homeschooling our children, each of us probably had a certain nuance as to why he chose this mission. For me, part of the "why" was an incident that happened years ago with my daughter at breakfast, and it reminded me of an incident written about many years ago.

Former communist Whittaker Chambers attributes the beginning of his conversion to Christianity with an incident of contemplating the complexity of his young daughter's ear, and thinking to himself that this delicate organ must have been formed by an intelligent and loving Being.

In his autobiographical book, *Witness*, he writes:

> My eye came to rest on the delicate convolutions of her ear—those intricate, perfect ears. The thought passed through my mind, "No, those ears were not created by any chance coming together of atoms in nature (the Communist view). They could have been created only by immense design."…Design presupposes God. I did not then know that, at that moment, the finger of God was first laid upon my forehead. (16)

Perhaps the Holy Spirit uses our daughters as a conduit to the gift of wisdom because I vividly remember a similar event in my life—seemingly insignificant, yet life-changing.

Years ago, while staring at my young daughter eating a Pop-Tart at breakfast, for some reason, I found myself pondering the idea that the devil not only wants *me* to go to Hell, but also wants to mortally wound the soul of *my little child*.

When I thought about the fact that the devils wanted *my* soul, that bothered me, but when I thought about the fact that demonic forces wanted my little daughter's soul, that angered me. Though I had always realized that I must protect all my children, I recognized at that moment that I must do everything in my reasonable power to protect her from *moral* danger.

Sometimes we fathers forget that. We must protect our children from moral danger as best we can.

That is one reason why homeschooling is so important. I've heard many fathers make good arguments *not* to homeschool. Some fathers are concerned that if they homeschool, their boys will not be able to play sports in high school. Some fathers argue that their wives are not capable of teaching certain subjects. Others are worried that their peers will think of them as outcasts.

Fathers must ask themselves: what is the goal for our children, and what is at stake?

In my years as an investment professional, I have worked with hundreds of Catholic parents. Many of them have adult children and some of them have told me heartbreaking stories about their children.

For the record, I have never heard a tear-jerking story about a child behind in Math class. A father doesn't say things like: "Mine is a tragic tale of woe…my son is a year behind in Algebra." A mother doesn't sob herself to sleep because her daughter didn't finish her Phonics 5 homework. I have never heard a distressing story about a boy not making it to professional soccer.

You know what the painful stories are about? One thing: their children have lost the Catholic Faith.

That's the heartbreak.

I believe in the power of grace, but as a Catholic, I also believe that God gives us free will. A parent can do everything right, and his children still may lose the Faith. However, we must take reasonable precautions to ensure that doesn't happen.

For many families, homeschooling is one of those ways.

I don't want to overstate the power of homeschooling. Regardless of what others tell you, it does not create a spiritual panacea. Homeschooling does not ensure salvation; it does not ensure sanctity; it doesn't even ensure a good education. For me, homeschooling offers one guarantee, and only one—it guarantees that my daughters will not sit in a classroom apart from their parents for six hours a day, five days a week, thirty-six weeks a year for twelve years. Homeschooling guarantees that one stranger after another does not teach each of my sons for the most influential twelve thousand, nine hundred and sixty hours of his childhood. Instead, I know that my children will spend those hours, those weeks, those years with one of the saintliest women I know—their mother.

For me, that is what is called in sales a "closer."

It is not my place to tell every father how to best meet the educational needs of his children, and I'm not suggesting that there are no Catholic schools that produce saints. On the contrary, the very existence of many universities is directly attributable to some great saints. And many saints were the products of formalized schooling, such as St. Thomas Aquinas, St. Bonaventure, and countless others. I personally know of a number of Catholic schools—led by dedicated staff and exceptional parents—that are doing an excellent job of primary education. They are to be congratulated. Clearly, for many families, the local Catholic school is not only a *good* solution—it is the *best* solution.

What I am suggesting is that if fathers feel called to the heroism of homeschooling, they should realize what's at stake, and accept the challenge. One day, each one of our children will stand before the judgment seat of Christ. When they do, it may not be the soccer that mattered, and it certainly won't be the Algebra. What will really matter is how they spent those thirteen thousand hours.

So fathers, when the going gets tough, remind yourselves why you're homeschooling in the first place. Try to remember, that whether or not you see yourself and your family traveling toward your heavenly destination, you're on the right path.

The Father's Role

As a financial professional who has assisted Catholic fathers with their family finances for almost a generation, and has given a number of motivational speeches to fathers at Catholic conferences, I have listened to the thoughts, feelings, and concerns of hundreds of fathers. These are great fathers, who have a loving concern for their children. Sadly, fathers like these are becoming more the exception than the rule.

In a society that is often lacking true masculinity, the need for authentic fatherhood has perhaps never been greater, but simultaneously, it has rarely been more absent. According to the National Fatherhood Initiative, 24 million American children live in a house apart from their biological fathers. But statistics like this don't do justice to the individual pain that boys and girls are suffering every day without having that father which nature intended for them. It is not the children who have lost their fathers prematurely who are suffering so much as it is those children who know that their fathers *could* be with them, but freely choose *not* to be.

Many of these men have been told that they were not needed anyway, so why stick around? The television show *Murphy Brown* infamously mocked the idea that a father is needed for a child, with the general support of the American press. In an effort to finalize the concept of "feminism" (perhaps one of the most mistermed words in the English language), many Western women attempted to throw off the constraints of paternal influence, and shattered their children in the process. In a culture that doesn't know how to, or simply refuses to define the word "family," the role of a father becomes seemingly insignificant.

Considering its real importance, very little is currently being written on the subject of Catholic fatherhood. To determine just how much had been written, I recently went to Amazon.com and did a search for the word "fatherhood," and a tagline appeared that read: "Did you mean motherhood?"

Not a good sign.

I then did a search on Amazon.com for "Catholic fatherhood." This produced 270 results. To establish comparative data, I typed in some other searches at random, and here are those results:

"Panda bears": 1,914 results.
"Black holes": 46,951 results.
"Applied Linear Algebra": 1,706 results.
"The number zero": 22,671 results.
"Welding theory": 284 results.
"Brazilian ecosystems": 153 results.

To use Amazon.com as a cultural indication, the amount written about Catholic fatherhood lies somewhere between the ecosystem of Brazil and the theory of welding.

This lack of writing on the topic of Catholic fatherhood leads to one of three conclusions: *first*, that fatherhood is irrelevant, and welding theory is actually more important; *second*, that fatherhood is so instinctive to men (kind of like breathing) that nothing *needs* to be written about it; or, *third*, that the idea of bettering oneself at fatherhood is inherently unknowable, and therefore, nothing *can* be written about it. Since a man can perform acts that more or less pertain to his children's welfare, the second and third possibilities seem impossible. The sad fact is that our society views fatherhood as increasingly irrelevant (at least in relation to welding).

In reality, however, fatherhood is critical, and one need not necessarily have a religious perspective to recognize this. As the authors of *The Unexpected Legacy of Divorce* write:

> After decades of minutely recording mother-child interactions as if they existed in a "daddy-less" world, researchers have finally discovered fathers and how important they are to a child's development. Today's answers to the question "What good are fathers?" would fill a small library. Children with sensitive, involved fathers surge ahead in their cognitive and social development as they explore their environment and play with other children.... And just to dispel the strange notion that fathers are more important to their sons than to their daughters, a study of young women who excelled in their academic studies at Stanford and Berkeley revealed they attributed their high ambition to their father's long-standing encouragement. In my own work on good marriages, I found that women who maintain a passionate relationship with their husbands throughout many years of the marriage had a healthy, loving relationship with their fathers as children. (Wallerstein 2000, 135)

One of the things that we Catholic fathers must appreciate is that our role is a major determinant for the entire lives of our children. There is a mountain of sociological and psychological evidence to support the claim that boys grow up either wanting to be exactly like their fathers or exactly *unlike* them, and girls try to find a man just like (or just *unlike*) their father to marry.

But there is a deeper, even more significant reality—a child's concept of God is often based on the father. Pope Benedict XVI examined this subject in his book, *Jesus of Nazareth*. The Holy Father, agreeing with Reinhold Schneider, wrote that the ability to call God "Father" is in itself an indescribable joy and great consolation. But then the Holy Father laments that, for many, the ability to call God "Father" is not a consolation, because it references a damaged or non-existent relationship. He writes:

> It is true, of course, that contemporary men and women have difficulty experiencing the great consolation of the word *father* immediately, since the experience of the father is in many cases either completely absent or is obscured by inadequate examples of fatherhood. (136)

It is often said that what homeschooling mothers need most from their husbands is support. But we need to demand more of ourselves than that. Yes, support is needed, but fatherhood must go beyond mere financial support. The relationship between a father and his children is not merely a monetary affiliation. Raising children does not mean handing them a paycheck. It means preparing them not merely for this world, but for the next. And it means being a positive influence in their lives. One author recently suggested that we re-define fatherhood, but fatherhood has already been defined. It has been defined by God. It needs to be re-discovered. It needs to be lived. Let that be our mission.

The Sound

Most Americans have heard Glenn Miller's music, but don't know the name of someone else who greatly contributed to his success. Though he had worked for years with some famous musicians, Glenn seemed convinced that there was a certain "sound" for which he was searching. Though insistent about his idea, he had times when he doubted himself, and considered abandoning his musical idea; however, he was blessed with someone who wouldn't let him give up on himself: his wife, Helen.

One family friend wrote about their marriage:

> But much as I liked and admired Glenn, it was to Helen that I gave the most credit for their happiness. In her own quiet way she was an immensely strong person. She would remain discreetly in the background, and yet, whenever Glenn had an important decision to make, he would turn to her, and she would help him. (Simon 1974, 49)

Without Helen Miller, who believed in her husband even when he had trouble believing in himself, the world may have never heard that "sound." Without her, couples may have never held hands and danced to the magnificent arrangement of *Moonlight Serenade*.

The homeschooling father plays a similar role to that of Helen Miller. First, he believes that his child has a sound that the world needs to hear. That "sound" may come in the form of a calling to the religious life, or to be a Navy Seal, an author, or a professional basketball player. Second, it is the job of a father to believe in his sons and daughters, even—*and especially*—when they don't believe in themselves. Third, the homeschooling father believes that it is his mission to help his son or daughter listen for that sound, and to recognize it when they hear it.

I have been a father for almost twenty years now, and I can think of many times when I have been involved in finding that sound. One such incident happened recently on a baseball field in Virginia.

Ever since my son Athanasius was a little boy, he has not been the "rah-rah" player that many coaches want on their teams. In a day and age that often puts more emphasis on style than substance, some coaches have overlooked him in favor of more boisterous players, even though he has often been statistically better than others. Though a confident young man, he began to doubt his baseball ability from time to time as a result of this oversight.

However, during his junior year in high school, Athan played in a homeschool baseball league for a coach that understood how good a player he was. In the final game of the year, the league championship game, on a cloudless spring night that was so perfect it seemed like an answer to a prayer, Athan and the other eight defensive players ran out and took their places to play a game that many of them will never forget.

Due to a combination of great pitching and good defense, the game was so close that you could almost feel spectators hold their breath on every ball and strike. The opposing team took a one-run lead early in the game and, for the ensuing three or four innings, it seemed like that single run would be the difference between victory and defeat.

In the top of the seventh inning, Athan had a collision with another player, which seemed to shake him up a little bit, but not enough to exit the game. Still, the coaches may have wondered if he were playing at his full potential. In the bottom of the seventh and final inning, as the sun seemed to be setting not only on northern Virginia, but also on their season, the team and the fans remained hopeful. After all, they had come from behind to win before, and it was *only* one run. It *could* happen.

The first batter of the inning had a walk. I, and probably many of the other parents were thinking to themselves something like: "OK, lead runner on. The odds of a lead runner scoring is about sixty percent. We've got a chance to tie this game."

The second batter got an infield hit. "We've got a runner in scoring position now. We can tie this thing!"

The third batter walked. Everyone in the park could feel the tide turning, as the players and fans began to sense that a hit of a good distance would not only tie the game, but win it.

The fourth batter made an out. No problem. There were still many ways to score that run from third with one out.

The fifth batter came to the plate: Athan Clark. Now I didn't hear anyone say it, but they must have been thinking it: "Wasn't this the kid that just had that collision? I hope he's OK."

First pitch. A ball outside.

Second pitch. The pitcher got the sign from his catcher, glanced at the runners, glimpsed back at his target, and hurled the little white ball toward the catcher's glove.

There is a famous poem, immortalized in the hearts of baseball fans, called "Casey at the Bat." The poet, Ernest Thayer, tells the fictional tale of a baseball game played by a team called The Mudville Nine. The author gives a sense to the reader that the citizens of Mudville had little else to cheer for in their little hometown other than their beloved team. In this particular game, the fans had all but given up hope, with their team losing by a score of 4 to 2, with two outs in the bottom of the ninth inning. But a glimmer of hope emerged, as back-to-back hits saw baserunners get to second and third base, and what *really* gave the crowd hope was that Casey—"mighty Casey"—the best player on the team, was coming to bat. Everyone in the crowd sensed that something momentous was about to happen, and even as Casey was down two strikes, they kept hope. The pitcher throws the third pitch, and Casey takes a thunderous swing. And this is what happens next:

> Oh, somewhere in this favored land the sun is shining bright,
> The band is playing somewhere, and somewhere hearts are light,
> And somewhere men are laughing, and little children shout;
> But there is no joy in Mudville—mighty Casey has struck out.

There may not have been joy in Mudville, but there was joy in Virginia. As the ball traveled toward the plate, Athan's vision and instincts told him that this was the right pitch, so he made a slight hitch backward with his hands, made a short stride with his front foot, and swung. There is a certain sound that a bat makes when the ball is perfectly hit. I don't know what this sounds like to someone who doesn't love the game—I've never been in those shoes. But whether the bat is made of wood or aluminum, when a baseball is hit perfectly, it sounds beautiful to a baseball fan. This is the sound that everyone heard that night, as Athan rocketed a line drive to the opposite field, scoring the two winning runs. A walk-off, 2 RBI hit. Championship won.

As the fans cheered wildly and as each player raced over to hug Athan, one thing was sure: he had found his sound. Athan and all my children, and all *your* children, have sounds to make not merely in sports, but in many areas throughout their lives. Every child has a sound within himself or herself. It is a sound given to each one of them by God. St. Albert the Great once commented that his most famous student, St. Thomas Aquinas, would one day bellow so loud that his sound would be heard throughout the world. Eight hundred years later, the "sound" of his magnificent mind can still be heard throughout the world.

A dear friend of mine, Father Constantine Belisarius, often says that God made each one of us because He thought that we were "a good idea." Though we all have a different sound, each of us members of the Mystical Body of Christ—each of the ideas of God—together compose a symphony, a *serenade* if you will, for the glory of God. We homeschooling fathers must pray that we are blessed with the grace and ability to help each of our children find that sound. That is how we find ours.

The Mercy of Fatherhood

It often happens that as a man gets older, he looks back on his life and worries about the sins of his past. As we get spiritually closer to Jesus, even though we know that Jesus has forgiven us in the Sacrament of Penance, it can bring us pain to reflect back on those occasions when we turned from Him. When we have these thoughts, it is imperative that we consider the Divine Mercy of Jesus.

In the 1930s, Jesus appeared to a Polish religious sister named Faustyna Kowalska, and revealed His message of mercy. As part of His message, Jesus explained that He wished a special feast to be established, during which souls may seek His special mercy. As St. Faustyna explains in her diary, Jesus spoke to her in these words:

> **My daughter, tell the whole world about My inconceivable mercy. I desire that the Feast of Mercy be a refuge and shelter for all souls, and especially for poor sinners. On that day the very depths of My tender mercy are open. I pour out a whole ocean of graces upon those souls who approach the fount of My mercy. The soul that will go to Confession and receive Holy Communion shall obtain complete forgiveness of sins and punishment. On that day all the divine floodgates through which grace flow are opened. Let no soul fear to draw near to Me, even though its sins be as scarlet. My mercy is so great that no mind, be it of man or of angel, will be able to fathom it throughout all eternity. (286)**

I've often thought that the receiving line in Heaven is composed not of the greatest saints, but of the greatest (repentant) sinners, as an eternal testimony to the unfathomable mercy of Jesus. Perhaps that is why, on the Confessional box at the Shrine of Divine Mercy in

Stockbridge, Massachusetts, a sign reads: "The greater the sinner, the greater his right to God's mercy." His mercy is for sinners.

If the thought of your sins begins to overwhelm you, remember that Jesus came to earth and suffered and died to save *your* soul. When Jesus was crowned with thorns, and was nailed to the Cross, and rose from the dead, He was thinking of *you*.

And this mercy should never be doubted. Jesus explained to St. Faustyna that He is sometimes hurt more by doubting souls who do not trust His forgiveness than by the sins they have committed. We should never doubt that the Passion and Death of Our Lord are sufficient to save souls. Because we might be tempted to doubt, Jesus gave us a prayer that we should say for the grace of trust, and it was very simple: "Jesus, I trust in You." Your sins may be great, but the mercy of Jesus is greater. Whenever you are tempted, say that little prayer.

There was another component to this message of mercy, and this is one that directly affects us as Catholic homeschooling fathers. The message of Jesus included that we should show mercy towards others. As Jesus explained to St. Faustyna:

> I demand from you deeds of mercy, which are to arise out of love for Me. You are to show mercy to your neighbors always and everywhere. You must not shrink from this or try to excuse or absolve yourself from it. (297-298)

It is important to Jesus that, just as He shows us mercy, we show mercy toward others. There are fourteen works of mercy, broken down into corporal and spiritual works of mercy. The seven corporal works of mercy are: feed the hungry; give drink to the thirsty; clothe the naked; visit the imprisoned; shelter the homeless; visit the sick; and bury the dead. The seven spiritual works of mercy are: instruct the ignorant; counsel the doubtful; admonish sinners; bear wrongs patiently; forgive offenses willingly; comfort the afflicted; and pray for the living and the dead.

You may not have realized it before, but if you wrote a description of the life of a Catholic homeschooling father, the list would pretty much look like this. The works of mercy are simply elegant ways of expressing the things you do every day. The last time you bought or cooked dinner for your family, gave your daughter a glass of iced tea, helped your son get dressed for Mass, said the Rosary with your children for the souls in Purgatory, paid your mortgage, helped your son with Phonics or Spelling, ordered a History book for your daughter, gave your wife a hug, or drove your children to Confession, you probably didn't think it was a big deal. But it *was* a big deal. It was then that you imitated Jesus. It was then that you were answering the call to be merciful. The works of mercy are the résumé of an authentic Catholic father.

St. Thérèse reminded us that sainthood is often achieved, not through magnificent works, but through a "little way" of serving Christ through others. Catholic homeschooling is often difficult, but we must always recognize the opportunity it presents. Every day is a chance to show mercy towards others, and often, we don't need to look far to do it.

Back in the Box

As a former college baseball coach and a lover of the game, I am frequently guilty of reducing life's greatest lessons to a series of baseball analogies. I often tell my children that if they fail at various trials in life, they have to be willing to try again and step back in the box. Normally, I use this expression figuratively. This time, I mean it literally. When we fathers fall into sin, we have to get back in the box—the Confessional box.

We are told that there is a crisis of the priesthood today—that there are not enough priests. However, if the only job of priests were to hear Confessions, we would have a huge surplus. What we have is a crisis of Penance. It appears as though the overwhelming majority of Catholics, especially men, are not using the sacrament of Penance anymore. If you have not made a good Confession in a while, you need to ask God for the grace to help you make a good Confession now.

The effects of *not* using the sacrament of Penance are brutal. A priest once explained to me that those things that *seem* to weigh us down—our financial troubles, American politics, our stresses at work—are not the things that are *really* hurting us. He explained that unconfessed sin weighs us down more than anything else, and that it creates a life of unhealthy fear and doubt. It creates a life in which we can't be honest with God. It creates an environment of unforgiveness. Our inability to forgive others is often a result of the fact that we refuse to be forgiven ourselves. It also creates an unhealthy family environment. My mother has mentioned to homeschooling groups that the reason we fathers must teach our children the Faith is that we want our children to go to Heaven *with us*. The other side of the coin is this: we need to go to Confession so that we can go to Heaven *with them*. But unless we are living a life of repentance, we might be headed for different destinations.

There is good news: Confession is a cure for the chaos you may feel. Peace awaits you, and there is a very simple prescription: get back in the box. It is not "too late." You are not "too far gone." You haven't made a good Confession for decades? God will forgive you. You've lived in mortal sin for fifty years? God will forgive you. Jesus revealed to one of the saints that even if you have more mortal sins on your soul than all the grains of sand in the world, He would still forgive a repentant heart. St. Faustyna wrote that she would confidently approach Jesus with repentance and sorrow, even if she had all the sins of the world on her soul, and expect His Divine Mercy.

If you haven't made a good Confession for a long time, going to Confession may be very hard for you to do. In fact, it might be one of the hardest things you've ever done. Do it anyway. The harder it is to go, the greater the satisfaction will be.

Many men feel uncomfortable going to Confession with their own parish priest. If you are uncomfortable with this, try another way. Call a priest in a different city and tell him that you haven't been to Confession in a long time, but that you want to set up an appointment to go to Confession. It's fine to admit to him that you are a little uncomfortable going to Confession.

By the way, the Sixth and Ninth Commandments are frequent topics in Confession. You are not breaking any new ground by confessing these sins. Not to make light of these sins, but in this day and age, priests are probably more surprised by men *not* confessing sins against purity than confessing them. Make the best Confession of your life. Make your Confession with the idea that this will be the last Confession of your life. If you do, you may realize that this is when your life really begins.

If you haven't been to Confession in a long time, what you have been missing is the peace that you need in your heart. A priest once told me that Jesus could have picked *any* way to forgive sins, but He chose a method that would grant us peace—by speaking to one of His representatives, and being comforted. Don't miss the knowledge of love and mercy that awaits repentant hearts.

Remember that Jesus is pleased with our repentance, and His infinite mercy awaits us. Jesus said to Saint Faustyna:

> **Tell souls where they are to look for solace; that is, in the Tribunal of Mercy** [the Sacrament of Reconciliation]. **There the greatest miracles take place** [and] **are incessantly repeated. To avail oneself of this miracle, it is not necessary to go on a great pilgrimage or to carry out some external ceremony; it suffices to come with faith to the feet of My representative and to reveal to him one's misery, and the miracle of Divine Mercy will be fully demonstrated. Were a soul like a decaying corpse so that from a human standpoint, there would be no** [hope of] **restoration and everything would already be lost, it is not so with God. The miracle of Divine Mercy restores that soul in full.** (511-512)

Are there any more consoling words in the whole world to a sinner? As fathers, we must help our children develop a habitual devotion to this Sacrament so that they know that the healing graces will always await them. What better gift can we give our children than exemplifying a penitential heart?

Hello, Good Men

When my oldest son, Athanasius, was about five years old, I observed him playing with his Star Wars toys, imagining a great battle of the good Jedi knights against "the bad guys." As I watched him play, I asked him: "Athan, if Jedi were *real*, who would be more powerful: a Jedi knight or Father John (our parish priest)?" Immediately, he answered: "A priest, because only a priest can change bread and wine into the Body and Blood of Jesus."

Athan's words illustrate a truth that we must always remember: in all practicing Catholic families, the role of the priest is so important that life without them is unimaginable.

We've heard a lot of talk over the past years about the "bad priests." The "bad priests" make news. In Hollywood, if a man runs away from his wife and children and remarries, he is often exalted. Divorced and remarried couples are fawned over, with every move reported, lest we miss a beat.

When a priest fails, he is attacked and immediately called a "hypocrite" by the media. This is not a new development by the liberal media—it has always been this way. St. John Vianney wrote that when people wish to attack the Faith, they begin by attacking the priests, since the role of the priest is vital to the Faith. Though they regard the priesthood as a sham, members of the media nevertheless hold priests to a standard that they would never hold for members of any other profession or state of life. This makes for a strange irony: even those who hate priests instinctively recognize the dignity of the priesthood.

Pope Pius XI called this a "tribute," writing:

> A last tribute to the priesthood is given by the enemies of the Church. ...(T)hey show that they fully appreciate the dignity and importance of the Catholic priesthood, by directing against it their first and fiercest blows; since they know well how close is the tie that binds the Church to her priests. The most rabid enemies of the Catholic priesthood are today the very enemies of God; a homage indeed to the priesthood, showing it the more worthy of honor and veneration. (30)

Priests are not endowed with a charism of perfection. Priests are men. They have temptations and weaknesses. We have every reason to believe that they are tempted more than laymen, although we also have every reason to believe that they receive more grace to assist them. They have bad days. They encounter unfriendly administrations. They must deal with the fact that the court of public opinion has passed sentence on them because of recent scandals. They are given accusatory glances by people who know nothing about them.

Yet they persevere. We husbands and fathers must learn from this perseverance. We fathers sometimes tremble at the thought of the responsibilities in our lives: our work, our financial responsibilities, our wives, our children. Priests are responsible for many souls in their care. We fathers need to learn this art of perseverance from priests, and pray for the grace of perseverance.

It is vital that we fathers teach our children the power and dignity of the priesthood. Children tend to marvel at the power of angels, but we should remind our children that, as many of the saints have observed, the priest possesses power that has not been given to a single angel in Heaven. St. Alphonsus Liguori observed that St. Michael the Archangel could chase away devils, but only a priest could absolve the sins of the penitent. All the saints in Heaven can pray for you, but only a priest can offer you absolution. No angel has the power to offer a single Mass. It has even been observed that the angels tremble at the power of the priest. St. John Vianney wrote: "If I were to meet a priest and an angel, I should salute the priest before I saluted the angel. The latter is the friend of God; but the priest holds His place."

We must learn to do something that we never do enough: thank the priests with whom God has blessed our lives. To those priests who may be reading this, speaking for myself and for many homeschooling fathers if they had the chance, *Thank you.* Your sacrifices are not in vain. By the grace of God, the souls of our children will be your trophies in Heaven. As pilgrims on this earth, your sacred vow to sacrifice the goods of a wife and children is what has given our families a home. Any spiritual success we have as Catholic fathers would be impossible without you. We cannot claim any victory that is not yours first. When our families are at peace, it is because you have granted us the consolation of the Sacraments. The love and dedication that you show Jesus inspires us. And please know that you are in our prayers, now and always.

A Prayer for Priests

Keep them, I pray Thee, dearest Lord,
Keep them, for they are Thine—
Thy priests whose lives burn out before
Thy consecrated shrine.
Keep them, for they are in the world,
Though from the world apart;
When earthly pleasures tempt, allure–
Shelter them in Thy heart.
Keep them, and comfort them in hours
Of loneliness and pain,
When all their life of sacrifice
For souls seems but in vain.
Keep them, and O remember, Lord,
they have no one but Thee,
Yet they have only human hearts,
With human frailty.
Keep them as spotless as the Host,
That daily they caress;
Their every thought and word and deed,
Deign, dearest Lord, to bless.

(*Pieta*, 67)

A Love Letter

Come to the Clark house around eight o'clock, and you will likely hear our family saying the Rosary. You also may hear children crying, Casey Clark (our kindly but ultimately boisterous cocker spaniel) barking, and a father asking his children not to mumble, but to speak clearly. If saying the Rosary in your house is kind of like ours—*chaotic*—you may be tempted to stop saying it, thinking that you may not be getting any graces from saying the prayers in this imperfect way. My advice: keep trying. But if you've gotten out of the habit of the Rosary, or never really got into the habit in the first place, let me give you some encouragement.

Whether the dog is barking, the kids are moaning, or the phone is ringing, we try to keep saying the Rosary. It would be nice to say the Rosary flawlessly, but prayers are almost never said perfectly, even by the saints. Don't take this the wrong way, but you may have never done *anything* perfectly, and if you refused to do anything that you couldn't do perfectly, you would drive yourself mad. In the entire history of the major leagues, there have only been twenty perfect games ever pitched. But a lot of men made a fine living by pitching imperfectly. For now, stop trying for perfect—just try for *trying*.

That doesn't mean you shouldn't try to do your best while praying the Rosary; it just means that when you have a family of little ones, your best may not look that great. But I have a feeling that in the eyes of God, it is magnificent.

The great Marian scholar, St. Louis de Montfort, commented that the Hail Mary prayer was:

> the most perfect compliment which you can give to Mary, because it is the compliment which the Most High sent her by an archangel, in order to win her heart...(158)

The recognition of the need to develop a personal relationship with Jesus has certainly been a beneficial area of theological concentration since the Second Vatican Council. But it must also be particularly stressed among *men*, and especially *now*, that it is vital that we men develop a personal relationship with Mary, the Mother of God.

As Pope Leo XIII wrote:

> And truly the Immaculate Virgin, chosen to be the Mother of God and thereby associated with Him in the work of man's salvation, has a favour and power with her Son greater than any human or angelic creature has ever obtained, or ever can gain. (2)

Mary has a tremendous intercessory ability—in fact, it exceeds that of all the saints in Heaven. What's more, she *wants* to help us. When Mary appeared to St. Catherine Laboure in 1830, Our Lady was standing on a globe, dressed in white, wearing rings with precious jewels that showed brilliant rays of light. She explained this vision to Saint Catherine:

> These rays symbolize the graces I shed upon those who ask for them. The gems from which the rays do not fall are the graces for which souls forget to ask. (Power-Waters 1990, 84)

Catholic fathers often say: "I don't say the Rosary. But I do say other prayers every day." What fathers need to recognize is that the Rosary cannot be compared with other forms of devotional prayer. The discussion of the Rosary has invited superlatives from the highest ranks. The Rosary has received unique praise from the popes, saints, and Mary herself for hundreds of years. As Blessed Pope John Paul II wrote:

> As a prayer for peace, the Rosary is also, and always has been, *a prayer of and for the family*. At one time this prayer was particularly dear to Christian families, and it certainly brought them closer together. It is important not to lose this precious inheritance. We need to return to the practice of family prayer and prayer for families, continuing to use the Rosary. (41)

It is not enough that you, as a father, simply issue a directive for your children to say the Rosary. You need to say it with them. As Pope Pius XI stated:

> The fathers and mothers of families particularly must give an example to their children, especially when, at sunset, they gather together after the day's work, within the domestic walls, and recite the Holy Rosary on bended knees before the image of the Virgin, together fusing voice, faith and sentiment. This is a beautiful and salutary custom, from which certainly there cannot but be derived tranquillity and abundance of heavenly gifts for the household. (28)

In short, what the popes and saints have taught us is that a Rosary said well is a love letter to the Mother of God.

In the time I have been giving talks on the Rosary, several women have mentioned to me that their husbands or fathers don't pray the Rosary with their families, but say their prayers silently and privately. This is a mistake. You might think that your faith is a private thing. It isn't. Your faith stopped being a private thing when you agreed to be a father. You must say it *aloud* with your children. Vocal prayer has been perpetually recommended by the Church, and was, after all, recommended by Christ Himself.

The impact of a child seeing his father kneeling down in front of Mary and praying aloud is powerful. It is an act of love and humility. It also teaches children a great lesson: the need to pray is a strength, not a weakness.

Strong men ask for Mary's help.

To encourage my little children to pray the Rosary, I ask that they remember my personal final judgment before the throne of Christ. When I stand before the awesome judgment seat of Christ, the devil will be there, providing a laundry list of reasons why I should not be admitted to Heaven. I tell my children that, at that moment, the devil will speak loudly. However, if my children are praying the Rosary for their father, Jesus will ignore the words of the devil. Jesus will say that He hears only the innocent prayers of children saying his Mother's favorite prayer, asking Jesus to have mercy on their father.

Fathers, when all seems bleak in your life, pick up your Rosary, and send a love letter to the Queen.

Before the Throne of God

In the homeschooling world, mothers' support groups abound, but I am unaware of an equivalent for fathers. Therefore, for the past few years, I have intended to develop a fathers' support group. The idea is not entirely altruistic; what I'm looking for is a place where I can share my concerns and thoughts, and obtain some encouragement for my state in life. Sadly, it has not quite gotten off the ground. If you're in my situation, consider that you already have a support group that you may not think about enough, and it exists in the person of St. Joseph. It is vital that we fathers develop a personal relationship with St. Joseph because we will find no better friend.

In some ways, the character of St. Joseph is very mysterious. The question is often asked, "Why is St. Joseph mentioned so little in the Gospels?" The Gospels do not record a single word spoken by St. Joseph. And yet, perhaps this lack of voice speaks volumes. St. Joseph listened carefully to God's agents, and then faithfully and boldly executed God's commands.

As Pope Leo XIII wrote in "Quamquam Pluries":

> Thus in giving Joseph the Blessed Virgin as spouse, God appointed him to be not only her life's companion, the witness of her maidenhood, the protector of her honour, but also…a participator in her sublime dignity. And Joseph shines among all mankind by the most august dignity, since by divine will, he was the guardian of the Son of God.…
>
> …he guarded from death the Child threatened by a monarch's jealousy, and found for Him a refuge; in the miseries of the journey and in the bitternesses of exile he was ever the companion, the assistance, and the upholder of the Virgin and of Jesus. (3)

The Church teaches that, as Mary is due a special veneration higher than that of any of the saints, called *hyperdulia*, St. Joseph is due the next level of veneration, called *proto-dulia*. St. Joseph is due honor surpassing that of all other saints except Our Lady.

That being said, there is a parallel between St. Joseph's calling and the calling of every Catholic father. We fathers are called by God to do much the same things that St. Joseph did: recognize *who* and *what* the enemies are, and protect our children from these forces and influences; be a loyal and faithful companion of our wives; support our families in a way that glorifies God; and recognize that the hardships that come with fatherhood help us on the road to perfection.

Men in history, including saints, are remembered for various things: winning a battle, governing a country, composing a symphony, writing a masterpiece, or inventing a life-changing device. St. Joseph did none of these. Even in his own time, in the eyes of the world, this small-town carpenter was insignificant. But St. Joseph's greatness did not lie in his business profession. St. Joseph's greatness and holiness were manifested in his relationships: husband and father.

You can spend your whole life searching through the want ads, but you will not find a job that approaches the importance of *your* job as a father. Your role as a father is more important than your day job—your fatherhood is more important than *anyone's* day job. You have been chosen to prepare immortal souls for eternity.

St. Joseph never looked outside his family for approval or for a sense of accomplishment—and neither should we.

Accomplishment is right there waiting for us.

You want to know what accomplishment looks like? It's the chocolate ice-cream-covered smile of a seven-year-old boy whose father took him out for dessert instead of catching up on some paperwork at the office.

It's the bright-eyed gaze of wonder of a three-year-old girl who turns the pages as her father reads *The Cat in the Hat* for the *fiftieth* time.

It's that confident look in your wife's eyes that says: "I know I chose the right man" as she watches you take your children to Holy Communion. You may never occupy the corner office, but you will reside in the hearts of those you love—and who love you. Meditating on St. Joseph should remind us that there really is no greater calling for us than fatherhood.

As the world beckons us to prove our importance, let's ask for St. Joseph's intercession, to remind us that there are no roles more important than the ones God has already blessed us with: fathers and husbands. As a husband and father, St. Joseph understands your anxieties, your pressures, and your troubles. Reverently speak to him as one homeschooling father to another, and humbly ask for his prayers.

Prayer to St. Joseph

O St. Joseph whose protection is so great, so strong,
so prompt before the Throne of God,
I place in you all my interests and desires.

O St. Joseph,
do assist me by your powerful intercession
and obtain for me from your Divine Son
all spiritual blessings through Jesus Christ, Our Lord;
so that having engaged here below your Heavenly power
I may offer my Thanksgiving and Homage to
the most Loving of Fathers.

O St. Joseph, I never weary contemplating you
and Jesus asleep in your arms.
I dare not approach while He reposes near your heart.
Press Him in my name and kiss His fine Head for me,
and ask Him to return the Kiss when I draw my dying breath.

St. Joseph, Patron of departing souls, pray for us. Amen.

(*Pieta*, 16)

Section 2: Works

Higher Learning

Though we homeschooling parents often like to imagine that the transition to college will be quite simple, college is not always the easiest adjustment for homeschooled students—at least it wasn't for me.

First of all, I had to be on time for class. When I was homeschooling during the high school years, there was no "on time." I rarely had a problem getting my schoolwork done, but I often did "pleasure" reading during school hours, and worked on Algebra at night. Philosophy class didn't work that way. Showing up fifteen minutes late for class is not the best way to endear yourself to the faculty. And leaving early isn't much better. I once asked my Composition and Rhetoric teacher if I could leave class early. She said: "I guess so. But why do you need to leave?"

"Because, Mrs. D.," I answered, "my attention span is nowhere near an hour and fifteen minutes." (Needless to say, I stayed for the entire class.)

But like it or not, you have to be on time for proper attendance credit. To me, this was also a new concept. My first day in class, roll call was taken, which I found pretty entertaining. Because I attended a rock-solid Catholic college, it seemed like almost all the girls were named "Mary" in some derivative.

"Maria?"

"Here."

"Mary Beth?"

"Here!"

"Mary Clare?"

"Here!"

"Lisa Marie?"

"Here."

I've never been good at remembering names, but Christendom College offered a significant advantage—if I forgot a girl's name, and called her "Mary," I had a pretty good chance of success.

I probably started a few conversations like this: "Didn't I see you in class? Mary, right?"

"No, *Maria*."

"Oh, sorry."

Second, being somewhat AD/HD (after all, I am male), I had a hard time sitting through some classes. Keep in mind, you're rarely forced to sit still when you're homeschooled. In fact, most homeschooled children don't even *own* a standard desk. (I didn't.) If you want to get up and walk around, you do it. When I was taking high school courses at home, I could listen to the *Christ the King, Lord of History* book on audiotape while I cleaned my bedroom or lifted weights in my basement. In college, most teachers frown on dumbbells in class (although it didn't stop me from attending). And the decoration is all wrong in the classroom. Like almost every kid who grew up during the 1980s, I had a poster of a red Ferrari tacked up in my bedroom/classroom. To me, that seemed conducive to educational inspiration. But at Christendom, no such décor.

Third, I found the lectures slightly difficult to follow, not because the teachers weren't good, but just because the lecture format was so new to me. On the first day of class, I had no idea how to be a college student. I saw students around me writing down things in their notebooks during lectures, but I hadn't a clue as to how to take notes. I may have decided right then that I had to teach my children how to take notes during lectures.

But the biggest difference—and I know this sounds blatantly obvious—is that there are *other* people in your class. That has both positives and negatives, but more than anything, it's distracting. Kids academically *ahead* of me (and that was much of the class), asked *questions* that I sometimes didn't understand, much less the *answers*. Kids academically *behind* me (an inauspicious few) asked questions that slowed me down. That didn't bother me—I wanted things to slow down. College holds a lot of promises, but few as certain as this—as soon as you graduate, you need to get a job. That's not the thought you want racing through your mind in Metaphysics class as you try to determine what is meant by "prime matter."

Even more distracting was the fact that there were pretty girls in class, and that clearly has its ups and downs (after all, I am male). Until that point, the best-looking kid in my "classroom" was my brother Paul. Coming from a family that prides itself on academics to such a high degree, I'd like to say I delved right into the scholastic life, but in truth, I spent the first few classes trying to figure out whom I wanted to date.

However, being homeschooled did offer me some big advantages when I got to college. Studying on my own came naturally—I had been doing that for years. I didn't have much use for study groups—in fact, I found them largely unproductive. And the fact that I had taken twelve years of *authentic* religion classes—in contrast to some of the students whose religion classes had been inane, if not openly heretical—significantly helped me.

By far, the writing that I had done as a homeschooled student was the most important asset that I brought with me to college. Writing papers was relatively easy for me, since my home education stressed it so much. This, coupled with the fact that I had excellent writing teachers at Christendom, helped me to love writing. At Christendom, I commonly helped other students with their papers. In fact, even as a sophomore, I was sought out by seniors who needed help and advice on their senior theses.

Although teachers often advised that a term paper should be started about six weeks before it was due, I commonly started term papers two days (or less) before the deadline. One exception I made to this was a paper I wrote for the recently departed Dr. Warren Carroll's *Communist Revolution* history class in my senior year. Being a huge admirer of the founder of Christendom College, I was bothered by the fact that I had never been as good a history student as my brothers who had preceded me, so I decided to really impress him. For this class, although the assignment called for a mere fifteen pages, I wrote a sixty-nine page paper on the topic of the Afghan War against the Soviets. When Dr. Carroll handed it back to me, he stood over my desk during class to tell me how well I had done. In the five courses I took with Dr. Carroll, the man who assured his students that "one man can make a difference," I was so proud to have him as a teacher. At least for that one moment, I think he was proud to have me as a student.

I hope he is still proud, as I'll always be of him.

The college life will offer new, exciting, and sometimes strange challenges to the homeschooled student. But all things considered, there are few better training grounds for higher learning than homeschooling.

Home (Schooling) Economics

It's no secret that most homeschooling fathers are seeking more time to spend with their children to help them with their studies, but many tend to fall short. It's a simple matter of chronology: twenty-four hours in a day, minus eight hours for work, minus six hours to sleep, minus half an hour to take out the trash, minus fifteen minutes to pick up the dinner at Five Guys Burgers and Fries, minus one-hour to watch a *Rockford Files* rerun. Let's face it—we're busy. But let me suggest an avenue that you might not fully appreciate yet: car trips. In our family, time spent in the car is used for informal classes. My car is frequently used for economics classes—a subject dear to my heart.

One school year, Athan had a violin class and Veronica had a ballet class in Winchester, Virginia, a city about thirty minutes away by car. Instead of listening to the radio, we often had a "class" in the Mustang. (And while it's not a Ferrari, a Mustang is nevertheless a cool place for a class.) The trip *to* Winchester was the lecture portion of the class, and the trip *back home* was the question and answer portion. On the way there, I would explain things like the Laffer Curve, and I would expect them to be able to explain it to me on the way home. That might seem a little informal, but you've got to remember that Arthur Laffer first explained his famous law on the back of a cocktail napkin.

I'd pepper my kids with questions like: "What's the difference between socialism and communism?" or "Why does private property produce a more efficient economy?" or "What effect does the devaluation of the dollar have on the Swiss franc?"

We also had a discussion about economic "goods." In economics, a "durable good" is defined as anything that lasts over a year, as opposed to a non-durable good, which lasts under a year. But this talk of durable goods sort of begs the question about geography, and by that I mean, does much of anything last for more than one year in a house with nine children? Economists might consider a lamp or a dish to be a durable good. Not in my house.

What about a power drill? That *would* be a durable good (if I hadn't loaned it out). A friend of mine likes to use the term "dumber than a bag of hammers," presumably meaning that you'd have to have a screw loose to carry around more than one hammer. Well, I have several hammers. They might be all I have in my tool box, but I proudly have several hammers. Hammers are durable.

This also gave me a chance to explain economics as it related to current events. For instance, I was recently driving Veronica back from her teen group and describing to her the latest Greek tragedy involving the Hellenic country going bankrupt. Rather than restructuring their sovereign debt, they could consider selling their country on eBay. They could describe it as follows:

> For sale: Greece. If you like coastal living, this is the place for you. Featuring especially strong "home defense" due to the area of Thermopylae, the gorgeous setting encourages a high level of philosophy (although the authorities won't react well if you get too influential among the youth). The culture is anything but atheistic: you want gods? We've got 'em. From Apollo to Zeus. We also have world-class olives. Place a bid or BUY IT NOW for $995. (Interesting trades considered.)

If you're going to live in my house, you're going to learn economics, whether you like it or not. And not just any economics—but *free market* economics. And, though this may sound odd, I view virtually any situation as a chance to illustrate the benefits of a free economy. (A friend once told me that I could discover a free market principle in a random episode of *Mayberry RFD*.) Case in point: I recently drove Demetrius, Tarcisius, Philomena, and Dominica to the pool. We had a deal that if they got their yard work and cleaning done that day, I would take them to the swimming pool. They finished their work, but by the time we got there, the pool had closed. We thought that the pool was open until seven o'clock, but we found out that it closed at five-thirty. This offended the children on the level of justice. It offended me on the level of economics.

As we walked back in the car, I used it as an opportunity to explain to the children the concepts of profit and loss. I explained that the rent and the maintenance were essentially fixed costs, which were unaffected by how late the pool was open, but that more income could, and should, be derived by the pool staying open much later. I then quizzed them on what the *variable costs* were to the pool, and they understood the concept pretty well. At least, two of them did. Demetrius and Tarcisius were interested in the economic side of the argument, but Philomena and Dominica were too hot to grapple with the esoteric concepts of finance. They just wanted to swim.

(The story does have a happy ending. We drove to another pool.)

There was a story in the news that one state in the union was considering capping the price of gasoline. Presumably, some of the legislators thought that this would be a good way of helping people cope with the high costs of driving. So I asked my son Athan, "If a single state put an artificial ceiling on the price of gasoline, what would happen?"

Athan answered: "The stores in that state wouldn't be able to sell gas because they couldn't afford to buy it, and people would have to travel to neighboring states to fill up their tanks. It's pretty obvious." I told him that it might seem obvious to him, but that's because we talk about economics all the time.

The fact that I choose to burden my children with economics doesn't suggest that *other* fathers should. Whatever subject you choose to concentrate on, try to use the time in the car to help children with academics. You might find that you not only help them with a school subject, but feel entertained as well. And you might be surprised how they incorporate their knowledge. One case in point: when Philomena turned nine, her grandmother gave her a twenty-dollar bill while I was at work. When I returned home, Dominica couldn't wait to tell me about her sister's good fortune, but Philomena didn't seem quite as excited. "What's wrong, Philomena? It's twenty dollars! That's pretty exciting, isn't it?"

She said, "Yeah…but it's only *American* money."

All this time I thought she wasn't listening.

A New Year

When I write monthly articles, I sometimes wonder how to inspire homeschooling fathers for yet another school year. I don't care how much you believe in homeschooling, you never look forward to Labor Day. When trips to the beach or to amusement parks give way to math books, pencil sharpeners, writing tablets, and flash cards, there's a note of sadness. So whenever I'm tempted to dread the thought of homeschooling, I try to remember why I'm doing it in the first place and what I like about it.

I like that on work days when I go home for lunch, all my children have lunch with me. I like watching Demetrius help Dominica with her reading. I like following the ups and downs of the continuing saga of Lisa helping Veronica with her math. I like giving Athanasius articles from magazines to edit. I like watching Bonaventure trace the letters A, B, and C with those enormous children's pencils. I like turning up the font size on my Kindle, and helping Immaculata sound out letters on the screen for the first time.

I like the fact that homeschooling directs me to be a better person.

When you are a homeschooling father, you are a significant influence on your children's lives. If you react well to that fact, it influences the words you use, the movies you watch, and the music you hear.

When Lisa announced that she was pregnant with our first baby, I put away The Beatles, Journey, and the rest of the rock groups that I'd rather not mention in print. I didn't want my children to listen to rock music, and I knew that if I did, they would too. I wanted them to like classical music, so I trained myself to like classical music. Now I go to classical music concerts, and I love them.

But music is only one area of our lives. There are many areas that have been quietly affected. As the homeschooling responsibility progresses, I try to go to Confession more, I say the Rosary more, and I think I have grown closer in my relationships with Jesus, Mary, and St. Joseph. Don't get me wrong—I'm not delusional. I know I'm a sinner like everyone else.

But the *desire* to be better is there, and my children, along with the choice to homeschool them, are largely responsible. A story may illustrate my point. We Eastern Catholics have always been fond of icons. These little representations of Jesus and the saints adorn our homes as constant reminders of Heaven. We believe that the icons on the walls help us to fight temptation because we don't want to commit sins which these icons will "see." At the liturgy, the priest incenses the parishioners along with the icons because we Catholics should be icons to the world, and should be a witness to others.

Lisa and I are fortunate, because we have nine little icons running around the house all the time.

I also like homeschooling because it seems to slow down the "growing-up" process. It seems like students at brick and mortar schools are always coming or going. I don't know about other fathers, but I feel like someone keeps pressing the *Fast Forward* button on my life. I guess it's better than pressing *Stop*. And just to continue the "my life can be summed up with a VCR" analogy, what I really want is *Pause*. I'm forty, which either seems really old (if you're a teenager of mine), or really young (if your name and face have been superimposed lately on a Smuckers Jar on the *Today Show*).

One morning before work, after making a Spiritual Communion with my children, I walked over to make the Sign of the Cross on Mary Katherine's little forehead, and she looked up at me and giggled. I remembered how much she looked like Veronica, now sixteen, at that age. It's been fifteen years but it seems like last week. Time has moved quickly, but the consolation is that I've been a big part of her life, and a big part of all the children's lives, not just in *quality* of time, but in *quantity* of time—an underestimated factor in child-raising.

I believe that time matters, and I think time spent with children has made me a better father. It is said that if a parent does his job properly, he becomes obsolete. As time goes by, I think the opposite is true. As a parent does his job better, he becomes more needed, and the children increasingly recognize the value of friendship with a parent who loves them.

What would my relationship be like with my parents if I had never homeschooled? I can't imagine we would be closer. It is said that no one, on his deathbed, regrets not spending more time at the office. Does any child regret not spending more time in the classroom? I doubt it. Homeschooling may be defined in many ways, but the simplest definition might be this: homeschooling is time spent learning with parents.

So instead of looking at each school year as just another nine months of chores, let's look at it as a "new year." Let's recognize the opportunity for prayers, works, sufferings, and joys that this year will bring. And embrace it.

Unknown Subjects

It's been almost thirty years since I was first homeschooled. Since that time, compared to most human endeavors, homeschooling has answered its critics so resoundingly that it has surprised even its ardent supporters. When my mother was promoting homeschooling thirty years ago, she couldn't have reasonably expected the level of success that homeschooling has achieved. It has gone from being a fringe activity to a mainstream one. During this time, I don't know if I've heard *all* the objections to homeschooling, but I'm confident I've heard *most* of them.

Among these objections:

"How will homeschooled children make friends?"

"How will homeschooled children get into sports programs?"

"How will homeschooled children get into college?"

Last but not least, my personal favorite: "How will homeschooled children learn multiculturalism?" (I lie awake nights worrying about this one.)

During the past generation and a half, most objections to homeschooling have been asked and answered. One objection, however, has proven especially resilient, namely: "How can a parent teach a child a subject that he does not know himself?" I'll call this the "Unknown Subjects Argument." When I first heard this argument as a teenager, it sounded like it made sense. It has a sort of metaphysical logic to it (i.e., "You can't give what you don't have"). I figured that some children need someone smarter than their moms or dads to teach them academic subjects. (Of course, I didn't think this applied to me; I didn't know any people smarter than my Mom or Dad. I still don't.)

However, as the years have gone by, I have realized that the Unknown Subjects Argument doesn't wash. The students *do* surpass the masters, and they do it regularly. Even my young children disprove the theory. For instance, when he was twelve years old, I took my son Demetrius to the National Aquarium in Baltimore and we toured the vast center, observing the fascinating sea life that God made on the Fifth Day.

A few weeks later, it dawned on me that Demetrius must have been more observant than I was. One night, Demetrius and I turned on *Jeopardy* just in time for the second round. I might have to confess the sin of pride for this, but I like to impress my children with how many questions I answer correctly. However, that night, a funny thing happened. The category of "Sea Creatures" was highlighted, and I was stumped on every question. Demetrius wasn't. In fact, he started running the category. "What is a white shark?" he answered. "What is a sea dragon?" he answered. The kid knows a lot about sea creatures. This got us into a conversation about mammals, fish, and marine biology. In fact, he informed me that he was thinking about being a marine biologist when he grows up.

If the Unknown Subject Argument were true, Demetrius' knowledge of marine biology would have been obstructed by the glass ceiling of my parental knowledge, but he has obviously surpassed my limitations. Because truth be told, the closest I've ever come to studying marine biology was a few Lents ago when I ordered the #4 Fish and Chips combo meal at Long John Silver's.

In reality, there is no glass ceiling that parents pass on to their children. Pope Pius XI recognized this fact, writing:

> For the most wise God would have failed to make sufficient provision for children that had been born, and so for the whole human race, if He had not given to those to whom He had entrusted the power and right to beget them, the power also and the right to educate them. (16)

"The power to educate them." Wow! Maybe we fathers ought to spend a little time contemplating this idea: that *we have the power to educate our children*. On a purely human level, one of the things that the Unknown Subject Argument fails to take into account is that educational methods have increased exponentially in the past thirty years. With modern technology, such as educational software, videotapes, CDs, DVDs, Internet sites, underwater web cams, online encyclopedias, videogames that teach children about sea life, not to mention books, magazines, and trips to aquariums, I have every reason to believe that Demetrius can use these tools to become a great marine biologist. He has already been doing a lot of this research on his own. Most importantly, he has a natural curiosity that drives his learning ability. The only glass ceiling in Demetrius' future is one on an aquarium tank.

I'm not embarrassed to admit that I know very little about astronomy, nuclear physics, or computer engineering, but I believe that my children could learn any of these subjects at an "A" level. I have no reason to believe otherwise. Moreover, this isn't just theoretical on my part. The evidence illustrates that many homeschooled children have gone on to establish successful careers in fields that their parents knew very little about. The Unknown Subjects Argument survives in theory, but fails in practice.

Just ask Demetrius.

Time and Tide

As a father, one of my responsibilities is to help my children stay out of trouble. But as the years go by, I wonder if it is the other way around.

One Saturday a few summers ago, I spent the day like a lot of other fathers were spending their days: getting my children to and from various activities. Athanasius was having a violin day-camp from 9:30 a.m. until 3:30 p.m. in one city; Demetrius had a baseball game scheduled at 1:00 p.m. in another city; and Veronica was having a ballet recital from 3:00 to 5:00 p.m. in yet another city. Clearly, I had some planning to do: getting three children to three different cities and watching all of their performances was going to be difficult.

So I grabbed my GPS, programmed in the various locations, and began to navigate and triangulate my driving path. As I did so, I began thinking back to—oddly enough—Saxon Math. When I was growing up, I used to complain to my mom about those bogus math problems like: John begins to drive his car at 3:00 p.m. traveling west at 60 miles per hour; two hundred miles away, Sam travels the opposite direction at 5:00 p.m. traveling 35 miles per hour; what time are they at the same location? I realized that having to drive around like this was my personal Dantean *contrapasso* for questioning my mom and her choice of math textbooks.

As I drove back and forth, watching my children undertake their various performances and playing my own version of *Beat the Clock*, another thought struck me: fathering keeps me out of trouble because it makes me use my time staying devoted to others.

Homeschooling is rewarding, but to say that it's time-consuming is an understatement. There's a saying in the sales profession: sales is the easiest poorly paying job in the world, and it is the hardest best-paying job. In other words, if you work hard, you'll probably do well financially, and if you don't, you'll probably struggle. Fatherhood is similar. To be a great father requires tremendous effort, and time.

Many men regard this time commitment as a negative. Don't. When you start lamenting the fact that you have no free time, remember this: what you lack in free time, you probably make up for in grace. Driving your child to a baseball game might consume an hour, but it improves you, your child, and the world. As I go to Little League baseball games, and ballet and violin recitals, I notice that many fathers are missing. No doubt, vital work commitments can prevent devoted fathers from being at events, but many fathers consider some things more important than watching their children. However, as a father, I can't think of a better way to spend an afternoon than watching my sons play or watching my daughters dance.

These things are supposed to occupy us as fathers—these are the things that are meant to use our time. There is a saying that an idle mind and idle hands are the devil's workshop. As a homeschooling father of nine, I have my share of problems, but being idle isn't one of them.

It's not just the dedicated time that helps you as a father, it's the dedication itself. Active fatherhood isn't just *time* consuming—it's consuming. Period. Being a father causes you to see things in a different way.

I don't know what it says about me that as a middle-aged American male, I don't have a favorite beer, but I *do* have a favorite brand of diapers (Pampers Swaddlers Supreme). I used to get excited looking at sports cars—now I save my "oohs" and "ahs" for eleven-passenger SUVs.

When I was at Mass a few years ago without my family, at the time of the Gospel, the entire congregation customarily stood. About halfway through the Gospel reading, I noticed I was doing something that must have seemed odd to onlookers: swaying back and forth. I have grown so accustomed to swaying while holding a small child in my arms while listening to the Gospel, I was now doing it without the baby. In a contraceptive world, I have reached a stage in which I feel out of place *without* children.

It may be true that "Time and tide wait for no man," but they are rewarding to those who use them well. It's hard to know what I'd be doing if I weren't a father. But I hope, believe, and pray that fatherhood is making me a better man. And, fathers, it is likely making better men of you, too.

For the record, Athanasius turned in a virtuoso performance of Haydn, Veronica enthralled the audience with her impression of classical ballet, and Demetrius had a successful at-bat in the bottom of the sixth inning.

And I was there for it all—right where I belonged.

It's a Wonderful Life

It seems no Christmas season is complete without a family viewing of the Frank Capra classic *It's a Wonderful Life*. But maybe we've never really considered the implications it has for us homeschooling fathers.

Unless you've spent every Christmas since World War II on Neptune, you know the story. It revolves around a man named George Bailey who spends his childhood dreaming of traveling the world and doing important things. Due to family circumstances, he is forced to remain in the little town of Bedford Falls to operate the Bailey Building and Loan Association. As the years go by, George sees his friends go live the dreams that he once had for himself. George finds that his life is devoted to the Building and Loan, not because he loves the business, but because he sees the good it can accomplish for others. However, one Christmas Eve, when money is missing from the bank, George is tempted to despair, commenting that things might have been better if he had never been born. George finds himself tearfully praying and asking God for help. God answers his prayer and sends him a guardian angel to show him what the world would have been like if he had never been born. In the course of this exercise, the angel shows George that many of the little things that he had done in his life made a profound difference in the lives of others. In the end, George realizes that he really did live a wonderful life, and his angel presents him with a message that reads: "No one is a failure who has friends."

What would life have been like if you hadn't homeschooled all these years? Unlike in the movie, it's hard to know what would have happened under different circumstances. But whether your desire to homeschool was born from the motive to protect your children from harmful influences or simply to give them a better education, it was love that motivated your decision. Most people don't homeschool for selfish reasons, and decisions that are motivated by authentic love are rarely wrong. They may be difficult, but they are usually correct.

The homeschooling father's life consists of acts that many people would consider insignificant: deciding to start a family and raise children instead of going off to pursue more worldly aspirations; choosing to enroll your children in an expensive violin or piano class instead of spending the money on a new car that might impress your friends; turning off an exciting football game at halftime on a Saturday afternoon in order to take your children to Confession instead; teaching your toddlers to say the Rosary. Whereas George needed to be shown that his life mattered to so many, we need faith to know that these things matter to our children.

George was determined to focus on his failings. The devils tempt us fathers to do that. They want to re-direct us from good works to worry about our failings and past sins. The devils want us to grow in fear rather than trusting in the mercy of Jesus. It's easy to focus on the negative: our kids are behind in math, our wives are overworked, we feel like we just aren't qualified to teach science as well as the local Catholic school teachers. We fathers are tempted to say to ourselves: "Maybe my kids would be better off if I had never homeschooled them at all."

In order to overcome these doubts, we must have faith. And we must remember that our faith teaches us that the smallest acts can contain tremendous significance. On one occasion last year, I was feeling a little depressed about something, and a father called and told me how much my articles meant to him. Let me assure you: *that mattered.* My son Bonaventure was once up with a cough, which meant that Lisa and I got very little sleep. So the following morning, I overslept and had to run out of the house without eating breakfast to get to work on time. My wife arrived an hour later at my office and brought me a blueberry waffle and a cup of coffee. *That mattered.* There have been times when you, as a father, were tired from the events of the day. You considered not saying the Rosary that day because everyone was so exhausted. But you said it anyway. *That mattered.* It mattered to you and to your family; it mattered to me and my family; and it mattered to the world. The rest of the world may not recognize it for a very long time, but it mattered.

Your decision to be a father, and your decision to homeschool, have caused a profound change for good in the world. Though I don't have my wings yet, let me assure you: it's been a wonderful life. My prayer is that you and I recognize it not just every Christmas, but every day. Because God already knows it. And although we probably won't have a direct conversation with our guardian angel anytime soon, perhaps if our guardian angel gave us a note this Christmas, it would read: "No man is a failure who has children."

Energetic Reading

When I began my professional career as an investment sage, my schedule was a bit hectic. I would leave home at 5:30 a.m., fight my way through traffic for about ninety minutes and arrive for work. Since I had no clients when I first started my job, I knew I needed to put in some serious hours, so I diligently worked until about 9 p.m. and left for home. At night, there wasn't much traffic—all the sane people had left for home hours earlier. When I finally walked through the door at 10 p.m. and called it a day—a sixteen-and-a-half hour day—I didn't have much energy left. At that time, Lisa and I had only one child, but I wanted to be present for him. Lisa kept him up until about 11 p.m. those days so he could see "Daddy" and play with me when I got home. The only energy I could muster was to take off my shirt and tie, throw them on the couch, and lie on the floor and let my little son climb on me, jump on me, and play wrestle with me on the carpet.

Even today, more than fifteen years later, though my schedule is closer to a more normal forty-hour work week, I often come home tired. The work hours may have dissipated, but so has my energy level. I'm guessing a lot of dads feel that way. Let's face it, after a long day, few of us drive home with excitement at the prospect of administering a history lesson to our teenagers. We fathers are tired. But as a homeschooling father, I still want to get involved with my children's academics, even if I'm out of breath from work. I was recently pondering this, and I kept asking myself, "What can I do to help my children with their homeschooling when my batteries are completely drained?" "What if I'm too tired to do *anything*?" Then, as I was perusing the nutritional information on the back of a box of Fruit Loops, the answer came to me: I can *listen* to my children read. It might take patience, but it doesn't take much energy. It's also a pretty good way to develop a love of reading for the children, and for the academic side of homeschooling, there is probably no better thing we can impart to our kids than a love of reading.

My mom had an ingenious plan to get us to read. I became aware of my mom's policy when I once asked her to let me stay up late and watch television, and she refused. "Your bedtime is eight o'clock, Johnny," she said.

I remember going to my oldest brother, Ken, who saw I was upset, and asked me what was wrong. Tearfully, I blurted out: "Mommy won't let me stay up and watch television."

Ken (perhaps in a foreshadowing of his future career as an attorney), suggested I speak to "Mom" and plead my case. Ken suggested that Mom must be unaware of a fundamental truth in American society. Ken said to explain to her: "Mom, prime time television is eight o'clock to eleven. I can't go to bed at eight o'clock. I'm missing all the first-run TV shows."

Though Ken had armed me with what, at the age of seven, seemed to me incontrovertible logic, she was not moved by my plea. However, she offered me a deal. I still had to go to bed at eight o'clock, but I could stay awake as late as I wanted as long as I was reading a book in bed.

Thus, a lifelong love affair with books was born. I used to read for one, two, and sometimes three hours at night. I read everything I could get my hands on—Narnia books,

Encyclopedia Brown, Tolkien, Hardy Boys, Bible stories. While the world was watching TV, prime time reading for me lasted from 8 until 11.

Though my mom's method was clever, and I have used it over the years for my own children, I have been trying my own system. We go to the library during the week when I have some energy, and help the children pick out books they can read throughout the week to me. I like the idea because it gets me more involved. It also helps me monitor what they are reading, which is good, because children's books are sometimes full of strange ideology. Demetrius likes to read about animals, but when I took him to the library to find a book about tigers, I discovered that the book we picked up should have been called *Environmental Brainwashing for Twelve-year-olds*. The author saw fit to include such "tiger-specific" topics as population control and global warming. At least if we read propaganda together, I can correct these notions as we go along.

So the next time you come home after a long day, have your children read to you. Better yet, pick up a book at the library that you will enjoy together, and have your child read it to you. Think of your children as a real life "books on tape" service. It will get your children reading, and you might find it more entertaining than you expected.

Checks and Balances

For most of my adult life, I have had my most important conversations around breakfast time. This seems to point to one of two possibilities: *first*, the restful sleep from the previous night has allowed me to start the new day with a fresh mind; or *second*, the effect of coffee brewed in my French press is so caffeine-laden that my mind is on the cutting edge of stimulus. I'm opting for the second choice, considering I haven't gotten a good night's sleep since 1993 (September 21st, to be exact). One recent morning was no exception. I was trying to explain the American government system of checks and balances to the children. I explained to them that the legislative, judicial, and executive entities work together to provide a system in which no *one* branch wields too much power. In the course of this, I was trying to find some kind of analogy that would help them understand this concept more clearly. Then it struck me: my family *is* a system of checks and balances.

Proudly, I am the executive branch. My wife, Lisa, would also constitute the executive branch, but she freely chooses to represent the legislative branch of our family. I think her public school education has made her a rebel: eschewing management power, she has more fun being the check and balance to the executive. She constitutes the legislative branch. And as the framers of our Constitution warned us in the *Federalist*, whatever precautions are taken, one of the branches would still have the most power. (I'm guessing you're already ahead of me.) Lisa makes laws which are never overruled by the executive branch.

My children are the judicial branch. Although they possess no formal powers of declaring the unconstitutionality of executive decisions, they nevertheless provide legal opinions of laws and the actions of the executive branch.

As an example, one morning I set my coffee down near the edge of the counter in my kitchen so I could make myself a waffle. Not unfamiliar to the sight of spills that have taken place under similar conditions, my seven-year-old daughter, Philomena, asked me, "Daddy, why did you put your coffee so close to the edge?"

"I like to live dangerously, Philomena," I told her.

Philomena thought about this for a minute as she watched me unsuccessfully attempt to pry, scrape, and chisel my waffle off my "non-stick" waffle iron, and then asked me: "Why do you like to live *dangerously*, Daddy?"

"I'm just kidding, Philomena. I don't *really* like to live dangerously," I responded.

Philomena, exactly replicating not only the *words* but also the nuance and inflection of her *first* question, responded: "Daddy, why did you put your coffee so close to the edge?"

You've heard it said that the U.S. Constitution is a living document. Well, Philomena is a living check and balance. She respectfully questions the wisdom of the executive branch. This is actually one of the great graces of having children. Most adults are too courteous or polite to question the decisions that other adults make. Children aren't like that at all—they don't even know *how* to be like that. An adult might have questioned why I put my coffee so close to the edge, but he never would have asked the second time. Philomena doesn't let me off so easy—she wants a logical answer.

As I continued the discussion about government with Athanasius, I also realized that not only does our family mirror the branches of government, we also have the equivalent of various government departments. "Mommy," I explained, "constitutes most of those departments." She heads the Department of Transportation, as she drives the children to baseball practice, ballet recitals, and violin performances. She also serves as the head of the Department of Agriculture, as she critiques my choices of fruit and vegetables when I return from the supermarket. (I don't look forward to those brutal inspections.) She has been in "labor" so many times that she is the honorary head of *that* department also.

We even have our own version of the Treasury Department. I came to this realization one Easter morning. My daughter Immaculata, who was one year old at the time, is *pascally challenged*, meaning that after ten minutes of hunting for about ten dozen brightly colored Easter eggs on a newly mown lawn, she was still unable to find any eggs for herself. And on Easter morning, there's really nothing sadder-looking than an empty Easter basket, except, of course, the expression on the face of the little girl holding that basket. So I went to speak with my other children, who had found their candy treasures, and attempted to reason with them.

I encouraged her brothers and sisters that, even though they found their eggs "fair and square," they should share the eggs with her. To their credit, they saw the charity in this action, and proceeded to provide her with an equal amount of candy from each basket. It impressed me that, even given the family math struggles of which I have previously written, my children can divide Easter candy with a level of precision that an electron microscope can only *envy*.

Although recognizing the spiritual value in their generosity, my daughter Veronica nevertheless voiced some concern that we had wandered off the free market path. "No, Veronica," I explained, "you have to understand. Immaculata is *too little to fail*. We're still a capitalist family—this is just *bailout* candy."

Now we are *really* echoing government.

Lost in Translation

In ancient times, the Egyptians, lacking an advanced alphabet, used a combination of pictures to express their ideas. That might amuse us in this day and age, but it seems that the Egyptians were actually *ahead* of their time. Teenagers have now adopted a similar system of communication.

George Bernard Shaw once observed that "England and America are two countries separated by the same language." I'm probably not the only father who feels separated from his teenagers by a common language lately—at least, I *think* it's a common language. I refer not to the English language, *per se*, but to what has come to be known as "text." For those uninitiated to "text" or "texting" (and you know who you are), it could be defined as a way of communicating by computer or handheld device which employs letters, numbers, symbols, or a combination of these. To account for this revolution, even the word "text" has undergone an etymological transformation. The word used to be a *noun*, as in: "Students, please study the *text* for next week's exam." It is now more often used as a *verb*, as in: "The way those jeans were ripped was, like, so cool; *text* me later about them," or "I'll be in Poly Sci class, so I'll have my ringer off—just *text* me."

Perhaps texting is the result of a generation of children who, faced with the prospect of taking years of English grammar courses, have decided instead to "opt out" of the system. Why study things like *singular-versus-plural* and *subject-verb agreement* when you can simply text and do an end run around the problem? Texting is heavenly bliss for the syntactically challenged. Like much of modern art, it is indefensible, but it is so bizarre that it transcends acceptable methods of critique. For instance, how can you "correct" expressions that contain an amorphous combination of dashes, parentheses, ampersands, equal signs, and numbers? Though they congratulate themselves on the creativity of text and symbolic expression, teenagers need to realize that this hieroglyphic form of communication is demonstrably confining. For instance, the English language contains dozens of synonyms for the words "happy" and "unhappy." But in text, there are precious few. In fact, there are essentially two: ☺ and ☹.

Parents are criticized as being unable to learn the language of their teenagers. I might stand guilty as charged, but when you write a would-be sentence which contains a happy face, a dollar sign, and a symbol meaning Abraham Lincoln, am I the one who can't communicate? I have actually had to "Google" certain texts to know what my children are trying to write. I'm guessing that, if you're my age (forty-something but, in my children's eyes, pushing octogenarian status awfully fast), some of you fathers have done the same thing.

Though our linguistic integrity might feel compromised, we parents need to learn this new odd dialect if we wish to communicate with our children. And if you're a writer wishing to attract a younger audience of readers, you're going to have to go along to get along. If Shakespeare wrote today, few would understand the sentence: "O Romeo, Romeo! wherefore art thou Romeo?" The Bard would need to write: "R, ? R U?" What it lacks in beauty, it makes up for in brevity.

Like it or not, we live in a text world. Case in point: the other day, I went with Athanasius to buy a *smartphone*. When you buy one, you are asked: "Do you plan on texting?" Not only do I not *plan* on texting, I hope that I am never *desperate* enough to "text." I look at it this way: there is poetry; there is prose—and then there is "text." Texting is among the lowest forms of communication. (I would say "the lowest" but I've worked in politics.) As opposed to standard typing, which employs ten fingers, texting is normally done exclusively with thumbs—and that's appropriate considering the results.

People today like to advise others that they must "think outside the box." However, if the "box" is the place where grammatically correct composition takes place, count me in. I like the box. I like the world of predicate nominatives, subordinate clauses, and proper punctuation. Reading "text" for any length of time makes me want to curl up with a good grammar book for relief. Sure, it may look a little strange reading *Warriner's English Grammar and Composition* over a cup of decaf at the local java shop, but I'm comfortable with that.

I can't believe I'm saying this, but maybe it's time we all took a refresher course on sentence diagramming. Maybe a good rule of thumb (no pun intended) is: "If you can't diagram it, don't text it." Can you imagine teaching a course on diagramming text? It would make for an interesting combination with the fact that teachers are often discouraged from giving the conventional A, B, C, D, and F grades these days. Teachers might return homework with notes such as, "William, the semicolon with a hyphen and a parenthesis means 'winking' which is a verb, so it goes to the right of ☺. Try not to make that mistake again or I'll be forced to give you a ☹."

BBIAB*.

* Be back in a bit.

Section 3: Sufferings

Fish Stories

About every two years, on those rare afternoons when we don't have any ballet, baseball, basketball, violin, or swimming scheduled, I say to my kids: "Why don't we go bowling? Bowling is fun." Two hours later, after breathing in a lung full of secondhand smoke, with my ears ringing from acid-rock-music-induced tinnitus, and wondering what sadistic mind it took to invent bowling shoes, I remember why it has been two years since we went bowling. (Note to bowling shoe makers: I would expect shoes to look and feel like that in a communist country, but certainly not here in America. Every time I put on bowling shoes, I feel like I am being transported back in time to Moscow during the Cold War.) Bowling isn't fun, but it takes approximately twenty-four months to *forget* that bowling isn't fun. (Right now, I'm on schedule to bowl again in November of 2013.)

On the drive back from a recent fishing expedition on Lake Erie, it struck me that fishing is like bowling. Mentally armed with the persistent notion that fishing is fun, I have promised my children that one day, I would take them fishing. So when my dad called me and asked if Athanasius and I would like to go fishing, I jumped at the chance. Athan deliberated as to whether he should go, but I assured him: "Fishing is fun!" I have determined that fishing is attractive to many men because there is something in the human male that likes to "rough it," meaning that we seek opportunities to do things the hard way. However, for American men of my ilk, "roughing it" consists of watching Wimbledon on anything less than a plasma high-definition television.

Four weeks after my conversation with Athan, as we arrived at our destination and walked to the front door of our cabin, we were greeted by approximately seven thousand ill-tempered mosquitoes, many of which were nice enough to follow us into the cabin. I swatted a few but quickly realized that the deck was stacked against us. They would come for us during the night. When you must apply bug repellent *before* you get into bed, you begin to question some decisions you've made in your life.

The next morning, as we departed at 5:20 a.m. and boarded the boat, I thought how fortunate I was that I was finally getting a chance to take my son fishing, and to relive some memories from my childhood with my dad. All my thoughts were positive: it looked like a perfect day for fishing. But this is where the rubber meets the road, or in this case, where the fiberglass meets the water. I had spent a lot of time on boats growing up, but I had never been seasick.

Until now.

The term "seasick" is a gentle euphemism which fails to adequately capture the essence of the illness. Motion sickness is the grand-slam of nausea. I could not remember feeling so nauseous in my life. I tried a couple of strategies to make myself feel better. I tried to stare at the horizon instead of the four-foot waves that rocked the boat. No luck. I tried to close my eyes and think happy thoughts about solid ground. No luck. As I sat in the boat on Lake Erie, or as I now refer to that body of water, "the River Styx," my thoughts turned to my wife. In her pregnancies, she has often been afflicted with morning sickness, which is very similar to motion sickness. Perhaps for the first time, I realized how much suffering she had endured in those times. I was impressed.

Still wanting to do something productive, I became the official person in charge of the net. Every so often, I would stand up and hand the net to the captain of the boat, who would capture the fish in his net. Here's a quick tip about nausea, and I consider this advice invaluable, so you might want to highlight this next sentence. When you are nauseous, it doesn't make you feel better to stand up and step into a box of rainwater and worms. I tell you this from experience. I hadn't packed an additional pair of shoes, so later that day, I went to a local sporting goods store in hopes of finding a new pair. As I swung open the door, I noticed a sign which read: "No shirt, no shoes, no service." The managers may have regretted that policy the moment I walked in the door with my shoes emitting a foul odor and leaving a trail of dirty water and crushed worms in my wake.

To add *insult* to my nausea, I caught no fish that day. I still don't understand how you can be *bad* at fishing. You put the worm on the hook, drop the line in the water, and wait. There doesn't seem to be much room for variance, yet ever since I was eight years old, my dad has caught exponentially more fish than I have caught.

As a father, you can't always filter out the bad experiences from the good. And I'm not sure we'd want to even if we could. It's both sets of experiences that give us character and make us who we are. As I get older I've begun to realize that *what* we do is less important than *with whom we do it*. And, illness aside, there are worse ways to spend a day than with your dad and your son on the water.

I'm just glad I'm on dry land again.

On Sleep

When I give talks at homeschooling conferences, newly married couples sometimes ask for advice. I'm impressed that these parents care enough about their responsibilities that even *before* having children, they investigate their educational choices. These parents are planners, and they're expecting some insightful information they can really use. "What should we do *now* to prepare for homeschooling in a few years?" they ask. They might consider my response somewhat flippant, insofar as it consists of a single word, but it's actually well thought out. In fact, I consider it profound.

The advice: "*sleep.*"

Socialist economists claim that wealth is a zero sum game. That is absurd (as if the level of wealth in the world has remained constant since year 1). But you know what *is* zero-sum? Sleep. There are twenty-four hours in a day, and there's nothing anyone can do about that. If you don't get enough sleep during these twenty-four hours, that's just too bad. I used to make fun of old people who fell asleep on the couch watching television.

Now I *envy* them.

Lisa and I have had an infant in the house for pretty much our entire married life. Let me translate what that means. It means that we haven't slept too darn much. If all goes well, babies sleep in three-hour increments—and it doesn't always go well. As others have observed, the term "slept like a baby" was coined by either a madman or an uninformed person. In reality, no adults sleep like babies, or at least, no adults I ever want to know. When you say that you "slept like a baby," it is a figurative term meaning that you "slept well." What it *literally* means is you woke up three times crying—*twice* because you wanted milk and *once* because you needed your diaper changed. That doesn't describe too many adults I know. The bottom line is this: being the parents of a baby, and getting a good night's sleep, are mutually exclusive pursuits.

But truth be told, infants are always getting a bad rap when it comes to sleeping habits. Older children can be *more* difficult. From about age three to seven, children are apparently stricken with what could be termed "dry mouth disorder." It is difficult to assign a medical explanation for this malady, since this thirst occurs only during bedtime. I can't remember the last time I was lying in bed as an adult, dozing off to sleep, and thinking to myself: "Hold on! I forgot to drink a huge glass of water." Yet, children become veritable camels at the drinking trough once their heads hit the pillow.

Children's nighttime bathroom habits also become the plague of parents, and by "bathroom habits," I don't mean the artwork done with AquaFresh on the lavatory wall (although that is a concern). One child of mine went through a six-month stage in which she felt compelled to tell me she had to go to the bathroom. She didn't need *help*—she just wanted to let me know she was going. Gosh, that's great to know at two-thirty in the morning. And, whatever my schedule for that day, Bonaventure went through a stage during which he would wake up at 6:45 every morning and play with Star Wars toys in his room—*complete with sound effects.*

Of course, morning habits are the things that happen after children actually *go* to sleep, which is no easy task. I have heard that there are certain inevitable laws in life, such as: "The hardness of the butter is directly proportionate to the softness of the bread." Here's another, which we can refer to as *Clark's First Law of Narcolepsy*: "Your children will be 'jacked up' in exact proportion to your tiredness." On those nights when you are especially tired, your children will be especially restless. I'm not sure why that is the case, but it must have something to do with the Fall of Man. My wife and I don't even ask questions like: "Why don't the kids just fall asleep once they get in bed?" That would be the equivalent of asking questions like: "Why don't people just knock on our door and hand us gold coins?" It's just not going to happen.

Every family has a different system for bedtimes. Not a single one of them works. Lisa and I have a system for deciding who puts the children to bed. Feel free to use it yourself. Here's how it works. It all started when we gave Philomena and Dominica a Nintendo Wii a couple of Christmases ago. One of the games that you can play on the Wii console is *Bowling*. Lisa and I compete against one another in Wii bowling, and the loser of the game puts the kids to bed. We call it "Bowling for Bedtimes." It might be more Biblical to cast lots, but I hate relying on pure chance.

It has become a family ritual, and the children stand and cheer for their parent of choice. The children who like to hear their father reading Dr. Seuss stories cheer for their mom, and the children who like to hear their mother sing to them at bedtime cheer for me. (Without revealing who usually wins, let's just say that if the kids hear one more reading of *Yertle the Turtle*, I might have a mutiny on my hands.)

So if you haven't had children yet, please take my advice to heart: sleep now, or forever hold your peace.

64 Degrees of Separation

Although this is hardly a newsflash to many moms, I have observed that pregnancy and hot weather don't mix. Several summers ago, my extremely pregnant wife, Lisa, insisted all July that the house remain at a steady temperature of 64 degrees—anything warmer than that was unacceptable to her. I felt for her—I really did—but in the summertime, 64 degrees felt surprisingly cold.

It was a little strange leaving my office, stepping out into a 99-degree day, driving home and then opening the door to my 64-degree house. Walking into my house was a little like drinking a Slurpee too fast. For the record, like many men, I'm usually hot even if the women around me are cold. Growing up, I could never figure out how my mother could wear, not one, but *two* sweaters—during *summer* months! My brothers and I used to complain about the heat, turn the fans or air conditioning on, and never give much thought that my mom had to go search for her sweaters. Boy, how the tables have been turned. I tried to explain this hot/cold problem to my wife, using examples like: "When you can't defrost meat in your own kitchen, it might signify a problem," or "Opening the refrigerator door actually *warms* our kitchen."

You also find yourself saying some strange things to your children, like, "Tarcisius, make sure you take off your sweatshirt before you go outside to play golf," or "No, Demetrius, we can't build a fire tonight."

I tried suggesting turning up the temperature to maybe 68 degrees, but my wife quickly reminded me of the golden rule of the thermostat: *those with the babies make the rules.*

Sixty-four degrees it was.

One night, when my wife and I were sitting with our kids watching *The Dick Van Dyke Show* (which brings us to the golden rule of the television: *those with the babies get the remote control*), something funny happened. Well, actually *two* funny things happened. The first was that, in the middle of August in northern Virginia, eight children and their father were huddling for warmth around a television, while the mother of the family sipped an iced tea. But the other thing was the question my wife asked. Right after Rob Petrie tripped over the ottoman in his living room, Lisa asked us: "Is it a little cool in here?" Keep in mind, when she asked this question, I had left a Wendy's Frosty on the kitchen counter, and after two hours, it had retained its essential chemical properties (to phrase that another way, for those non-chemists reading this: *it was still frozen!*). Actually, that part of the story is embellished—I would never leave a Frosty unattended for two hours.

Through semi-chattering teeth, I was able to get out a response to Lisa's question, "No, honey, it feels about right to me."

"Really? It feels a little chilly. Must have been a draft," she replied.

"Yea, must have been a draft from outside," I answered.

It was like living in a meat locker—the problem is, we couldn't cook any meat. We weren't allowed to use the oven—it made the house too hot for Lisa. Before that, we used to have biscuits in the morning, but cold cereal became the norm. In fact, we collected so many toy surprises from cereal boxes that summer that it became the Clark version of "Christmas in July." Since I couldn't use the oven, I ordered so much pizza that summer that the local pizzeria owner started to treat me like a family member.

Of course, these weren't the only downsides. My utility bill was interesting, if not frightening. I could just imagine employees at the power company passing around my electric bill before dropping it in the mail, making comments like: "Hey, Frank, look at this—what do you think Clark's doing over in that house?"

I can tell you what I was doing—freezing. That year, I couldn't wait for summer to be over and be warm again. People say that babies bring warmth to a family. In our case, it was literally true.

You might be thinking that this has caused some contention between my wife and me. However, nothing could be further from the truth.

With my wife, I know how good I have it.

I've thought that on the day of my judgment, I will stand before God and He will ask me what good I did on earth. My response will be: "I loved my wife." God will pause for a moment and say: "You married Lisa McGuire. How hard was that?" After nearly twenty years, eleven pregnancies, ups and downs, hots and colds, richer and poorer, and all the rest, I can still make a claim that few men can make: I married my dream girl.

I just wish she liked it a little warmer.

Decaf

During a medical exam I took a few years ago, my physician recommended that I cut coffee from my diet. With the emotional roller coaster of the financial markets and my wife tampering with the thermostat, he apparently considered my life exciting enough without the added caffeine stimulus. This was no minor suggestion, as coffee had come to represent a significant facet of my life.

With the myriad of coffees, macchiatos, syrups, espressos, and double shots, some people are intimidated to go to coffee bars. I'm not. I'm the one you want to go with. Even with all the choices available at a typical shop, I routinely order "off the menu" and guide the baristas how to produce arabical brilliance in a cup. Over the years, I've become what is called a "coffee snob." I smugly dismiss those who call themselves "coffee drinkers," yet have the temerity to drink supermarket-bought coffee. I once found myself insulted when I brought a bag of coffee beans to the checkout at my local coffee store, and the woman behind the counter asked me if I wanted them ground (as if I didn't own a coffee grinder!!!). I've even given serious consideration to roasting my own coffee beans.

Suffice it to say that giving up coffee was not exactly something that I had planned on doing. (And there is some question as to whether the local coffee shop would have expanded if they had known.) But since my doctor assured me that I could still drink decaffeinated coffee, I thought I would give it a try. Specifically, he recommended that I cut my caffeinated coffee intake by one-half every few days until eliminated to zero. I assured him that this was a mathematical impossibility, but trying to be a "spirit of the law" kind of guy, I played along.

So the next day, I went into the local coffee shop and ordered a "half-caf with half and half," although I quickly discovered another mathematical formula: one-half plus one-half plus one-half equals one: *one headache*. As the following days wore on, I noticed something else: it's a bit emasculating to order decaf coffee. Nobody's proud to order it. In terms of masculinity, ordering decaf coffee lies somewhere between ordering diet soda and non-alcoholic beer. If you order a Diet Coke, people consider that a wise decision. If you order decaf coffee, people wonder what's wrong with you. So you start saying the word "decaf" in kind of an under-your-breath, or throat-clearing way: "Could you make that a (cough) decaf?" It's probably still better than ordering a near-beer, but not by much.

Even my daughter Veronica informed me that making decaf coffee is against her religion. (Yes, she's Catholic.) And if you think about it, she has a point. It seems unnatural. You're drinking something, but it's based on a lie. You tell yourself that you're drinking coffee, but you're not open to all that coffee has to offer.

As the following week ensued, and my headache started to dissipate along with my caffeine intake, a funny thing happened. I didn't need coffee any more. I used to get coffee headaches, meaning that if I didn't have a cup of coffee by ten o'clock in the morning, I'd get a headache. Getting a good cup of coffee every morning, regardless of circumstance, is not always an easy thing to do: sometimes it is almost impossible. Some days, it's not fun to race to the coffee shop—it can be a real inconvenience. But a week after my coffee purge began, I noticed that I no longer needed it.

Because my beautiful, oft-pregnant wife has turned me into the kind of person that finds a spiritual meaning in any circumstance, I began to recognize something: this coffee story serves as a microcosm of Christianity. Eventually, we have to give up attachment to everything—everything except God. Before we can meet Christ, we have to free ourselves of all those things that separate us—habits, thoughts, sins. We have to desire what the Sacred Heart of Jesus desires… and nothing else.

It's not the coffee that gives you freedom—it's the absence of the *need* to drink coffee that gives you freedom. Now it's certainly not a sin to drink coffee, and there are many things that are worse than coffee. Recent medical findings even suggest that there is some benefit to it. But that's really not the point: the point is that attachment to so many things must be surrendered. In the Eastern Liturgy, we pray for the grace to "set aside all earthly cares." This prayer signifies that it's not just the sins that often hold us back, it's the worldly things that may not be sins, but may be distractions, whether it's golf, television, or the Internet.

Maybe the lesson is that we must "decaf" our lives. If it won't be in Heaven with us, maybe we should stop paying so much attention to it now; and if it will be in Heaven with us, maybe we should pay more attention to it now. There is no Internet or television in Heaven, but there is love, there is family, and there is God.

Fathers, as the homeschooling moves along, remember that the sacrifices you make are for those things and those people that will be with you in Heaven. Let's all pray that we remember that lesson when things get hard.

And please pray for me for strength when I pass Starbucks.

Long Division

There are times when I consider myself so disorganized and so discombobulated that I think I must be the wrong person to write about the father's role in homeschooling. Sometimes I ask myself: "If people were aware of the fact that I often have Fruit Loops on my kitchen floor, would people still read my columns?"

It doesn't help matters much that, apparently, I'm not all that academic myself. I was once trying to explain to my daughter how to do "long division," only I ran into a slight problem: I couldn't actually remember *how* to do long division. I can calculate a bond yield, figure out the payment on a car loan, or determine how early I can pay off a mortgage by paying an extra $50 per month, but (and please don't tell anyone) I cheat. I have this thing called a "calculator." You may even have one yourself. And, if I remember correctly, one of the initial reasons I bought a calculator was because I didn't ever want to do long division problems again.

But there I was, attempting to solve this problem. Perhaps sensing my agony, my wife asked if she could see the problem I was working on, and proceeded to solve it herself in under sixty seconds. When you're about forty years old, there are few things more emasculating than watching your wife doing your long division homework. Furthermore, when your mother is Mary Kay Clark, you're expected to know basic arithmetic. I felt like I should call one of the math counselors at Seton the next day and confess that I had a small problem: I was twenty-seven years behind in math.

With all the children, from an organizational perspective, life is a little dicey. When my wife has morning sickness, I take over a number of domestic responsibilities. Incidentally, I'm not sure who coined the phrase "morning sickness," but apparently he or she had never met my wife. There's really nothing unique about the morning, except for the fact that it signifies yet another day to be sick for eighteen hours. When she is pregnant, my wife Lisa is almost constantly nauseous, and not the type of nauseous you get when you look at a batch of long division problems—I mean *really* nauseous.

Lisa cannot be around food when pregnant. For those of you who are blessed with better math skills than myself, you've already figured out that, over the years, I have done quite a bit of cooking. That is not good news for those of my children who actually *like* food, which is most of them. Truly, I'm not that bad at cooking, although the children look forward to Frito pie maybe more than they should.

I also help with the vacuuming and mopping. By the way, are vacuums *meant* to be disposable? Maybe it's a generational thing, but I have this strange notion that anything with an electric cord is *not* disposable. They are constantly breaking in my house. Right now, I have two vacuums sitting in my garage, as a testimony to this fact. They are also a reminder of the fact that I'm not too great at fixing things.

I took over the laundry detail, which produced its own set of rules. I once heard about a family that had a rule that *any* two socks were considered a "match." I don't blame them. When I was growing up, we had a "socks box" which was a cardboard box that my mom dumped clean socks into so we boys could attempt to find a pair. Even though at any given time the box contained a hundred socks, we were largely unsuccessful. I don't believe in many conspiracy theories, but here's one I could really warm up to: sock makers, hoping to spur continuous demand for their products, produce socks that are *similar*, but variant *enough* that people are unlikely to classify the two of them as a match. What other explanation could there be as to how it is possible to accumulate *nineteen* black socks without having one match? In any case, with me in charge of the sock helm, this rule has been slightly amended: any *one* sock is a match. (If God graces us with a tenth child, we will consider adopting a fashion rule made popular in the mid-eighties: no socks should *ever* be worn.) (By the way, please forgive the fact that I've been writing parenthetically so much. The truth is, I've been doing *everything* parenthetically lately.)

Now, fathers and rhetoric teachers alike, you've been waiting patiently for a thesis statement. Here it is: in homeschooling, as in life, the principal virtue isn't organization—it's perseverance.

The Random House Dictionary lists two definitions of perseverance. The first definition reads: "steady persistence in a course of action, a purpose, a state, etc., esp. in spite of difficulties, obstacles, or discouragement." But it is the second definition that interests me. It reads: "continuance in a state of grace to the end, leading to eternal salvation."

A life of homeschooling has taught me a valuable lesson: perseverance is the undercurrent of love, and love is the undercurrent of perseverance.

Perseverance is making dinner or doing laundry so your wife can get a little extra rest. Perseverance is helping your daughter with her division, even if it means that you have to re-learn subjects so you can teach them better. Perseverance means continually accepting the grace you are given to love those entrusted to your care.

Perseverance is the grace of realizing that today is a new day to know, love, and serve God by knowing, loving, and serving others.

And so is tomorrow.

Fifty

My mother recently had surgery, after which she was confined to a hospital room for several days of recovery. Because the hospital was about sixty miles away from their house, my father stayed in a nearby hotel so he could spend nearly every waking moment with her in her room. However, since my father's leg amputation, he often has trouble getting from place to place himself. He, too, needed help, in order to get back and forth to the hospital to see his wife.

After he had spent about twelve hours in the hospital with my mom, he asked me if I could help get him back to his car and over to the hotel. As he turned his wheelchair toward the door, he stopped to say goodbye to my mom. Seeing that his wife was in pain, he hoisted himself up from his wheelchair, and balancing on one leg, leaned precariously over her hospital recliner, and gave his bride a kiss. Maybe I'm getting soft in my old age, but I thought that was pretty cool.

Romance media may be enthralled with the weak-kneed feeling that young teenagers in love often have for each other, but it was the single weak-kneed balancing act that my father did that day which impressed me. On June 17, 2011, they celebrated their fiftieth wedding anniversary. And if you're a homeschooling family, whether or not you realize it, this merger that took place back then represents an important part of *your* life, too—perhaps not for the first twenty-five years of their marriage, but certainly for the second quarter-century.

For the first generation of their wedded bliss, it was raising children that defined their union. There may be a father who is prouder of his sons than Bruce Clark, but I've never met one. And the woman you know as Dr. Mary Kay Clark was once known to Ken, Kevin, Daniel, Paul, John, Jim, and Tim Clark simply as, "Mom."

And though they have never wavered in their roles as parents to the children who love them (I still go to them for advice before just about anyone else), for the past two-and-a-half decades, it has been homeschooling that has defined their marriage. The notion of homeschooling was novel back in the early 1980s, but in the same way that an artist envisions the finished sculpture in a formless piece of rock, my mom saw potential in this radical new form of education—this "homeschooling." Though she was involved in education prior to directing Seton Home Study School, it was as though my mother observed a world in which Catholic families were hurting from the results of spiritually harmful educational choices, and said to herself: "There must be a better way."

And then she found it.

The name Mary Kay Clark will forever be associated with Catholic homeschooling. When I think of the influence she has had in the world, it is staggering. She has, with the assistance of many devoted men and women over the years, helped change the world for the better through Seton—one family at a time. She has directly assisted thousands of families (and indirectly assisted perhaps hundreds of thousands) over the years—by showing parents how to teach their children, but more importantly, by helping parents believe that they *could* teach their children, and that home is where they belonged. In a world growing increasingly hostile to basic values, she has helped parents find a way to retain their children's innocence through home education.

My father, a former Green Beret, police officer, novelist, semi-professional baseball player, orchestral music arranger, concert musician, business consultant, and whose IQ is legendary, now identifies himself with a single moniker: "Seton historian." My dad loves few things more than explaining the fine points of history to homeschooled students. Many conversations with my dad in my adult life have started with: "The other day I was speaking to one of our kids…" That's what he refers to the Seton history students as: "our kids." The fact that he references them as such gives rise to another point of academics, and one that is often missed: reading, writing, and arithmetic are more adjective than noun. In other words, the basic focus of education should be on the child. Since its earliest days, Seton has managed to do just that: keep the spotlight on the child.

When you consider that my mom was voted as one of the most influential Catholics of the Twentieth Century, what's also impressive is this: she and her husband are not done yet—not by a long shot. They believe that they have much more to do to glorify God in this life, and I have no doubt that this is what they will do. When my father was in college, a priest taught him that if there is a difference between the *talent that God gave you*, and *how much you use that talent to glorify Him* then you are cheating God—and God should never be cheated. This has become their living motto—yesterday, today, and tomorrow.

It would be hard to strike a better balance between raising one's own children and assisting other parents in raising theirs than what we've seen from Bruce and Mary Kay these fifty years. And raising seven boys may have been the best possible preparation for their current roles. Perhaps as their son, I have observed something that no one else has considered. They have labored in an apostolate in which they sought to strengthen other people's marriages, and a funny thing happened—it strengthened *theirs* in the process. The self-giving that Matrimony calls for is present in their daily lives, and its merits have caused their relationship to grow increasingly wondrous. May it be so for many years to come.

May it be so for all of us.

In worldly terms, this marriage is going into its latter stages. But seeing the balancing act of that kiss, and the roles that they have played in this world, one is more inclined to think, not of time, but of eternity. And in that sense, the springtime of romance will always be in bloom.

No Rest for the Weary

When you're growing up, you can always count on your mom to help you feel better when you're sick. Moms just instinctively know how to help their children. It has been said that no thermometer is as accurate as a mother's hand. There is a lot of truth to that saying. Moms seem to be able to "feel" how well or how sick their children are in a way that surpasses the limits of mere medical instrumentation. When I was sick as a little boy, my mom used to buy me throat lozenges, make soup for me, comfort me, and reassure me that I'd be out playing with the other boys very soon. If I had a fever, she would bring me cool washcloths to put on my forehead to bring down my temperature. If I didn't feel like reading, she'd let me lie on the couch in front of the television, where I could enjoy the best game shows that the 1970s culture could muster: *The Price is Right*, *The Joker's Wild*, and *Tic Tac Dough*. With my mom in charge of my recovery process, I knew I would get better. Though I may have been ill, this level of attention made me feel like a king. In fact, when you're little, there's probably no time in your life that you feel more protected and more pampered than when you're sick.

Sickness is a little different when you're forty. First of all, my mom is at work. And that's not good, because like my wife always says: "It doesn't matter how old you are, whether you are four or forty, you still want your mom when you're sick." I'd like to call my mom and let her know I was sick, but since she's helping thousands of Catholic parents educate their children, I'd probably feel guilty asking her to drive over to my house with some Sucrets.

When you're a parent of nine, getting sick is a luxury you can't afford. This became apparent to me recently when I succumbed to the ravages of winter. What you'd like to do when you're "under the weather" is to lie in bed, have someone bring you lots of fluids, fluff your pillows, and generally maintain a quiet atmosphere, conducive to getting healthy. Reality doesn't work out quite that well.

Children like to "check on" sick parents—usually when those parents have finally been able to fall asleep. Example:

Child: "Daddy...*Daddy*...Daddy?"

Father: "Yes, sweetie. Are you OK?"

Child: "I'm fine. Mommy wants to know if you are asleep yet."

Daddy: "Tell Mommy I'm fine. I'll feel better soon, and then we'll play with your Pet Shop Toys."

Child: "OK, Daddy. Have a good sleep."

Rinse and repeat in one hour.

Children *do* seem to want to do their homeschooling near their sick parent. When I was lying in bed recently with the flu, seven-year-old Dominica and nine-year-old Philomena came in with their violins and music stands and proceeded to practice the new classical pieces they were learning. It was truly a wunderkind performance, but competitive violin and nausea don't mix.

When children have disagreements that need officiating, and they need the wise advice of a parent, they are faced with a question: "Should I ask the healthy parent or the sick parent?" In this case, the sick parent is suddenly viewed by the children as King Solomon. Only the sick parent who is lying in bed seems capable of answering disputes of titanic importance that have a clear immediacy, such as: "Which of us did Daddy buy the magenta crayon for?"

When you're eight years old, you don't go back to school until you feel better. When you're forty, and you decide to get up and go back to work, it's not necessarily because you're feeling better—it's because you've reached the stage in which you realize that you're not going to get any better by lying in bed.

There are few things in life that make you feel more special than a little three-year-old coming into your room with a concerned, slightly sad look on her face, asking you if you feel better, and wanting you to play—even when you'd rather be sleeping your way to recovery. But this bout with illness got me thinking that perhaps Lisa and I should incorporate a nursing class into our homeschooling regimen. Maybe as Seton considers adding new courses, parents can suggest that they add the class. Maybe it can be written by moms to show the non-mom populace how to take care of people.

There is another lesson I've learned. When you are a father, it is much better to be sick *yourself* than to see one of your children sick. As a father, seeing a child suffer with illness has never been easy for me. I doubt it's ever easy for most fathers. I'm sure many of us fathers, upon seeing our sick children, have prayed that we could suffer in their place. I think that this is just a prayer of instinctive fatherhood.

One thing I *have* decided with all this—the next time I'm sick, I'm calling my Mom.

Television and Lent

Around Ash Wednesday every year, many homeschooling families revisit their annual question: "What should we give up for Lent?" While there are many worthwhile answers to the question, there may be no better candidate than television.

Those of my parents' generation might comment that this would be no big loss, since television is so bad today anyway. They might ask: "Why can't television be like it used to be, when it was good?" Of course, there's a problem with this question, because truth compels one to admit that television has *never* been that good. True, the 1950s introduced some good shows such as *I Love Lucy*, *The Jack Benny Show*, *You Bet Your Life*, and *The Twilight Zone*. Then again, it gave the world *Kukla, Fran, and Ollie* and *Search for Tomorrow*.

From its earliest days, television was a victim of its own design. Hours of programming were forced into the otherwise-dead airwaves. It didn't matter whether the programming was worth watching or not; something—*anything*—desperately had to occupy these time slots. This fact was not lost on everyone. An FCC Chairman once commented that if you sat down to watch television, you would see

> ...blood and thunder, mayhem, violence, sadism, murder, western badmen, western good men, private eyes, gangsters, more violence, and cartoons. And, endless, commercials—many screaming, cajoling, and offending. And most of all, boredom. (Minow 1996, 188)

These comments were not made in 2011—they were made in 1961.

When you consider shows like *The Beverly Hillbillies, Flipper, The Munsters,* and *Gilligan's Island,* you get his point. I understand that they're not attempting to do Shakespeare quality, but these shows fail in comparison with the less-than-exacting standards of a Little Theatre casting call.

There has always been a clamor for more children's and family shows, but when I was growing up, these shows were not that good, either. Granted, the puppet government in the "Neighborhood of Make Believe" on *Mister Rogers' Neighborhood* gave American children a healthy introduction to the concept of monarchy, but King Friday was a bit too authoritarian for my taste.

Little House on the Prairie was a family favorite in the 1970s, but to say that I found it depressing would be an understatement. I'm probably going to get some hate mail for writing this, but I don't let my children watch the show. It's brutal. For the uninitiated, here's a recap of the show: Charles breaks his ribs falling from a tree; the Ingalls family gets swindled out of their cattle; a hailstorm ruins the family crop harvest; Charles attempts to sober-up his drunken friend; workers are blown up with dynamite; Laura becomes irate that her family dares attend a funeral instead of her birthday party; a rabid raccoon terrorizes the family chickens; Mary starts a fire in the family barn; the Ingalls' newborn son dies; most of the citizens of Walnut Grove are struck with typhus, which kills many of them; the Ingalls' dog is run over by a wagon; once again, Charles must attempt to rehabilitate an abusive alcoholic; Charles almost dies of hypothermia.

That's season one. Somehow, the family survived another eight seasons or so—at least most of them did.

"But these shows are harmless," you may say. Maybe, but watching television not only consists of what you *are* doing, it also consists of what you *aren't* doing. The irony of "family shows" is that they are programs about other people that take away from the attention that you might otherwise be giving to your own family. In America, some fathers have a deeper "friendship" with fictional television characters than with members of their own families.

"But if I give up television, how will I get the news?" you ask. "I need to know what's happening in: Zimbabwe/Estonia/Panama" or "I have to find out how that thing with: the Republican Party/the new state law in Arizona/the Acai crop in Brazil turned out."

Aren't we all "newsed-out" anyway? The news is often nothing more than a collection of the stories of the sins of others that we have no business knowing in the first place. And I don't mean tabloid television—I mean mainstream news. "But I need to watch the news to know for whom I should pray," some argue. However, for hundreds of years, the Church has been blessed with orders of nuns and monks who prayed for the world while knowing little, if anything, of what was happening in it. Ask yourself an honest question: When was the last time that I felt uplifted after watching the news?

Television offers a variety of shows, so it's not fair to lump it all together and conclude that television is all good or all bad. After all, EWTN is on one channel while soap-operas are on the other. But Lent is a good time to reassess the priorities in our lives. If you're seriously addicted, try to take at least an hour off a night from television, and help your family devote this sixty minutes to God.

In one hour, you can lead your family in the Rosary, you can say the prayers that were written by St. Bridget of Sweden about the Passion of our Lord, and you can say the Stations of the Cross. At the end of this hour, you will feel uplifted, and you will have helped your family take one more spiritual step toward the celebration of the Resurrection of Jesus. That is time well spent.

Mere Fatherhood

About a decade ago, I spoke with a Catholic nun who had been providing hospice care for the dying for many years. As we spoke, I commented to her that it must be depressing at times to be in the midst of so much death, and wondered how people spent their last moments on earth. Her comment to me was simple and profound. She said, "People die as they have lived."

Thomas Vander Woude, who was a pioneer in the homeschooling movement, being for a brief time director of Seton Home Study School, spent sixty-six years showing those around him how to live, and on September 8, 2008, he showed us how to die.

On that day, Mr. Vander Woude's twenty-year-old son Joseph (who has Downs Syndrome, and is the youngest of seven boys), fell through a septic field cover into a deep tank which was almost full. Seeing what had happened, Thomas ran toward the opening and tried to pull his son out of the tank from the top. Quickly realizing that pulling Joseph out was impossible, Thomas then climbed down into the tank himself, through the mucky water, past his son, and lifted his son up so the boy could breathe, until help arrived fifteen minutes later. Mr. Vander Woude was able to save Joseph; however, due to methane gas poisoning, Thomas was pronounced dead moments later.

The worldwide response to this story has been overwhelming. His Requiem was attended by over two thousand people, seventy priests, and about one hundred altar boys. Mr. Vander Woude's heroic actions have been talked about on the floor of the U.S. Senate, preached about in churches all over the world, and written about in newspapers in a number of countries.

Father George Rutler wrote a book a few years ago called *A Crisis of Saints*—lamenting the fact that so few saints are in our midst. I've no reason to doubt him, but his comment makes me recognize that I've been graced in my life to know men and women who love Christ so much and so well, and certainly Thomas Vander Woude was one.

Mr. Vander Woude was an accomplished man: he was a Vietnam veteran, a pilot, an educator, a sacristan, and a beloved coach. But it was his final act of heroism that defined him as a husband and father. In the end, Thomas Vander Woude heroically gave his life to save his son—but he'd been doing that his entire life. To honor him properly, we must recognize that his heroism didn't *start* on September 8th—it simply reached its high point that day. His life and death also go on to illustrate something that men often forget: while we fathers search for ways to better the world, the one that makes the most difference is the daily practice of authentic fatherhood.

Mere fatherhood is enough.

In the years since his death, people who knew Tom have related incidents about how he affected their lives: the families he sacrificed for, and the churches he volunteered for. The players he coached have come forward with stories about the impact Thomas had on them. I have one such story myself.

I didn't really get to know Tom until about four years before the accident. He served as the athletic director at Christendom College for five years, during which he made it known that he was looking for a coach for the Christendom baseball team. Although I've never played the game well myself, I've always been passionate about baseball, and I had good success coaching my sons in Little League for two or three years. When I heard there was a job opening, I sent Mr. Vander Woude a letter explaining to him that I'd like the job. What I *didn't* tell him was that it was my dream job. The idea of coaching my alma mater's team in my favorite sport was enthralling. However, the reasons *not* to hire me were obvious—starting with one rather striking deficiency: I had never coached anyone over ten years old.

A few days later, Tom called to tell me that he had picked me to coach the Christendom team. I will always remember that phone call. Although I was happy with his choice, I expressed some surprise that he had picked me because of my lack of experience. But he didn't allow me to doubt myself; rather than harp on what I *hadn't* accomplished, Tom insisted that I recognize the things that I *had* accomplished. He believed in me—he made me believe I was better at coaching than I was. I think he believed that if he expressed confidence in me, sooner or later, I'd grow into it.

Only after his passing did I realize what he was doing—he was coaching me how to be a better coach. More importantly, he was coaching me how to be a better father because I realized through his instruction that coaching is so much like fathering. He never referenced his achievements to make a point, which he very easily could have done. In the two years I coached under him, he never questioned a decision of mine—and he easily could have.

He did everything within his power to help others succeed. Working within the confines of a small Catholic college and a budget to match, the problem was how to practice—with no baseball field, no batting cage, not much of anything. But he was determined to help us succeed. We couldn't afford to buy a commercial batting cage, so he designed a batting cage for us, drove to the hardware store to buy the parts, and after coaching his last basketball game of the season, and after his players left, he stayed in the gym and built the cage with us.

In my rookie game as the coach, to the surprise of almost everyone (including me), our team won against a school about three times larger than ours. I remember calling Tom afterward to tell him we had won. When we spoke, his voice was elated. And yet, he didn't seem surprised—he almost expected our achievement. Your first win as a coach is something that you never forget, and he made that win possible.

I think Tom cared about sports because he recognized that sports offered a proving ground for men—it's a place for men to have a chance to excel, and to have a chance to *fail*. Coaching at Christendom was not all about success (although he had his share of those); it was more about how to fail, and *get back up*. I think he believed that sports served as a microcosm of the Christian life—it's not so much the batting average that matters, it's how many times you step into the batter's box and try again. Or as he might have put it, it's how many shots you take.

Tom and I spoke about two weeks before the accident, and, as usual, we talked about sports, we talked about coaching boys, but I never got the chance to tell him something that I always should have: any man who has sons like his must be a great father.

It's always difficult to write about someone who has profoundly affected your life. I need an angelic vocabulary, because words like "heroic" and "courageous" don't suffice. Maybe the best way to express my thoughts and gratitude is to say: I'll be a better *coach* because I knew him. I'll be a better *father* because I knew him. I'll be a better *man* because I knew Thomas Vander Woude.

Maybe that's the highest tribute I can pay.

Section 4: Joys

Eight Isn't Enough

On September 25, 2009, my wife and I were blessed with our ninth child on earth. Shortly thereafter, I tried to sit down and write about the experience. But as I attempted to describe the event, I couldn't help thinking about the time when I first became a father. Back in 1993, as my wife lay in her bed a few hours after giving birth, cuddling our own newborn son, Athanasius, I went into the bedroom and found her crying. I asked, "Lisa, the baby's fine; you're fine. What's the matter?"

She looked at her new baby, gently resting in her arms, and blurted out: "One day, he's going to leave us."

I smiled and consoled Lisa with the reality that it would be quite a while until that happened. "He'll be with us for at least eighteen years, sweetie," I assured her. "You'll have a lot of time with him until then."

Eighteen years have passed. The idea of a child leaving home is theoretical at age two. It's a reality at age eighteen. That's when panic sets in. "Have we taught him enough? Have I prepared him adequately for a world that is hostile to Catholicism?" In the homeschooling world, grades are given out to students all the time, but the parents are given the most important grade the moment their children step out the door. All parents probably go through this, although no one ever warned me about this moment. The consoling part is that, as important as the parents are to the family, we are not *all-important*. I believe that God will always be watching my children and granting them graces, and just like accepting a new life requires faith, so does letting children go require faith. And in the grand scheme of things, we never really let our children go. Hopefully, the family Rosary we say every night is a precursor of speaking to Mary in person as a family in Heaven.

In the meantime, we fathers must enjoy the presence, the innocence, and the experience of our children. I know that I am living at a time in my life that I will later refer to as "the good old days." I know there will come a time when I would pay a million dollars to travel back in time to have the pleasure of reading *The Cat in the Hat* to Philomena and Dominica in their Christmas pajamas. I'll miss taking Veronica to the shoe store downtown to pick out pink ballet slippers. I know I'll miss hugging Bonaventure and feeling his sticky fingers on the back of my neck. I'll miss playing computer golf with Demetrius and Tarcisius on the XBOX. I'll miss singing to Immaculata before bedtime. I know I'll miss the gentle cooing sounds of Mary Katherine (or "Baby Kay" as the children call her) while she lies in her mother's arms.

I even get the idea Lisa will miss the physical demands of mothering. There are days that she, like most moms, feels exhausted, but after a certain point, the athleticism required to raise children becomes part of a person's character. Considering that one of the most rigorous things Lisa did as a teenager occurred on fashion runways, the energy that Lisa has devoted to her maternal life is extraordinary. Ponder this: in our nineteen years of marriage, my wife has been pregnant and/or nursing for all but *eleven weeks*. That's dedication.

I'll also miss homeschooling my children: giving them history quizzes, checking their math, or asking them what they learned in their science books. All those things that seem inconvenient to us fathers now will mean so much later. These moments that occur in our lives should remind us fathers that we need to be generous with our time in the lives of our children.

Speaking of generosity, over the years, some Catholics have complimented Lisa and me for our generosity: the generosity of having children. But when I looked at Mary Katherine, accidentally smiling as she drifted off to sleep, the last thing on my mind was *my* generosity. It is "the generosity of God," as Father George Rutler once phrased it, that is overwhelming. For God, eight wasn't enough. As I think about what God has blessed me with, mine is an embarrassment of riches.

But this comment about generosity has made me appreciate my own parents and the generosity they have shown to their children, and the generosity they have shown God: taking the time to teach us the Faith, enjoying time spent with us, and homeschooling us. Our recent addition has left me thinking about how many times I've missed the opportunity to pray for my own parents, in the way that I want my children to pray for me.

We fathers need to pray for our parents more. One friend of mine in particular has taught me a lot about praying for our parents. In the years I've known him, he has gone to Mass almost every day to pray for his father, who passed away much too soon. It's the quiet kind of spiritual heroism we should all practice for our parents, and that we too often forget. Forty years, nine children, and two parents who love me have taught me that you never stop being a father, and you never stop being a son, or in the case of Mary Katherine Siena Clark, a daughter.

Forty

When I was turning forty, I thought it would be a good time to jot down some of the lessons I had learned in life. You would think with four decades under my belt that I'd have a lot of wisdom to impart, but the following will have to do anyway.

1) It doesn't matter how you start—it's how you finish.

It's an old saying, but it's true—how you finish is a pretty important part of the equation. Referencing the fact that he had run from God for many years, and only later in life did he enter the Catholic Church, St. Augustine lamented to God: "Late have I loved thee." Although we may have done it in different ways, we have *all* loved God late. But the hope of sinners is that God is not looking at the *lateness*—He's looking at the *love*.

2) Forgiveness is a lifelong process.

Whenever I think of someone who has crossed me or done or said something mean to me (either in reality or in my imagination), I get out a sheet of paper and write down ten things about him that are good. I might list things like: "God loves him" and "He says the Rosary," or "He works hard to provide for his children." By the time I get to the sixth or seventh attribute, I begin to realize how stupid I have been not to have forgiven him sooner. By the way, I've never finished a list. I've never needed to finish one. I also pray for something else. Other people may have had to make a list about me, and I ask God that they will have a special grace to forgive me.

3) **If you want to have a better marriage, love Jesus more.**

Since I was married when I was 21, I've spent roughly half my life married. And I know it sounds strange, but I don't remember clearly what it feels like to *not* be married. Actually, I may remember what it's like, but I just don't want to remember. A life without Lisa is too difficult to ponder.

In college, after Lisa broke up with me (all together, I think she broke up with me three times), a friend tried to console me by saying that "there are other fish in the sea." I told him, "You don't understand. You don't 'get over' Lisa McGuire." And I wouldn't have. The fact that I find Lisa stunningly attractive is not what makes this marriage work. It's the simplicity of her love of Jesus—not the beauty of her face—that has been a main ingredient of our marriage. How do you thank someone who has taught you to love Jesus more completely?

Good marriages don't signify that you never argue, or that your spouse always looks good. (If it did, I would be in trouble. There's a reason I don't include a picture in my columns.) Good marriages indicate that the love of Jesus is the centripetal force that powers that union. When my spiritual life is going well, my marriage is going well. And I'm guessing that this applies to pretty much everyone.

4) **Children are expensive, but the payoff is massive.**

As a parent who has had three children simultaneously in braces (a record for my orthodontist), let's stop trying to dance around the fact that having children is expensive. Don't let that ruin your day. A lot of people put off having children because they "need to invest for the future." Let me tell you something: having children *is* investing for the future. The most important investment is life itself. The sooner the world learns that, the better off it will be.

5) Childlike wonder is the best kind.

One morning, before I left for work, it began to snow for the first time of the season. In my house, "snow" is known as a four-letter-word. I have a litany of reasons not to like the powdery substance, not the least of which is that it has to be cold to snow. ("Cold" is another four-letter-word.) As my mind raced with reasons to be depressed, I heard seven-year-old Dominica from upstairs gleefully proclaim: "It's snowing!!!" We adults spend so much time trying to convince ourselves that everything is a tragedy, whereas little children spend their days finding silver linings. The world would be better if we all operated that way.

6) God never quits.

Author Francis Thompson wrote a poem called "The Hound of Heaven" in which he describes God as a loving Being who constantly pursues those He has created. Even when we run from God, God never gives up the search. Thompson writes:

> I fled Him, down the nights and down the days;
> I fled Him, down the arches of the years;
> I fled Him, down the labyrinthine ways
> Of my own mind; and in the mist of tears...

I have run from God many times through sin or lack of trust. We all have. But God never ran away from me—and

He never ran away from you either. He has been with us all along, patiently waiting for us to accept His love. As I begin my fifth decade on earth, my prayer is that I stop running.

7) **Kindness is the solution.**

In a book I wrote about economics from a Catholic perspective, I argue that the main problem of economics is not greed, but envy, which could be defined as "sorrow for another's good." I further argue that the solution to economics is kindness, which could be defined as the "joy for another's good." Kindness is never wrong, but rarely practiced, at least by me. It would be helpful if we all pick ten acts of kindness to practice, and make them habits. As Willy Wonka reminded us, kind deeds shine in a weary world. The next time you bake, make an extra pie for a poor family or for your soup kitchen. Say a Hail Mary for one stranger every day. It might be the first time that anyone has ever asked for Mary's intercession for that person in his entire life. Think about that.

8) **Homeschooling means having a conversation with your child, and that's a pretty neat thing.**

It might be a twelve-year conversation, and it might be about geography and history, but it's a conversation nevertheless. By the way, for those of you having a hard time homeschooling, remember that it was once much more difficult for parents, and much more awkward for their kids. There is a song called "I Was Country When Country Wasn't Cool." I'm proud of the fact that I was homeschooling when homeschooling wasn't cool.

9) Every day is a chance to love God more.

Don't chase big things your whole life and avoid small things along the way. The rest of my life may have dramatic moments of loving God, but most moments will probably occur in the form of seemingly small things, such as turning the pages of a book, playing Scrabble with my kids, or watching snow fall.

10) I am the luckiest man alive.

Recently, it's with particular understanding that I view Lou Gherig's comment about being the luckiest man alive. We all should feel like that, and I'm ashamed for times I haven't. God came down from Heaven and died on a cross for me because He loves me. The doubt we sometimes have springs from our inability to see things clearly, and to view them as a puzzle.

When I was a little boy, my mom used to buy me puzzles. I remember opening the boxes and seeing various pieces which, by themselves, made very little sense. I would struggle to find the piece that fit into another. It takes patience to build a puzzle, along with the faith that the right pieces are in the box. One by one, I would patiently put the pieces together until the magical moment when I'd finally begin to recognize the picture that I had been assembling. From that point on, putting the puzzle together was easy—the pieces just became easier to find. There have been times I've doubted, but after forty years, the puzzle is becoming clearer to me. The times that were the hardest—the ones that seemed least likely to fit—were the times that made the puzzle great.

After forty years, I have never been more sure of my unworthiness to be with God, but never more sure of God's Holy Will to save my soul. Everything has aligned so perfectly: the family to which I was born, my parents, the girl I married, the place I live, the friends that God put in my path, my children who constantly remind me of God's love and mercy, and the priests I have known. Each person's path has been different, but each person's path is meant to lead to God.

Love Story

Whether it comes in the persons of Odysseus and Penelope, Romeo and Juliet, or Jamal and Latika, from the ancient Greeks to modern times, every society has glamorized love stories. But one of the greatest love stories I ever saw didn't take place in the movies, and it didn't take place in books. It took place in my parish church.

This love story occurred between a husband and wife in their sixties who were longtime parishioners. A few years before he died, the husband was struck with Alzheimer's Disease. Even as an outsider, to witness the Alzheimer's process unfold is difficult. It would be inhuman not to feel a sense of pathos, not only for the one who suffers from Alzheimer's, but for those who love him or her. The victim gradually loses more and more of his intellectual abilities until he becomes like a child. The hardest part is that its sufferers forget all those around them—their friends, their own children, and their husbands or wives. One can only imagine the emotional devastation of a man or woman who is forgotten by his or her spouse. In a sense, it is the memory that determines who we are, and without it, we are lost to ourselves and to those dear to us. But those who love the victims of Alzheimer's endure.

The wife would arrive early to church with her husband, and would always sit up front with him, perhaps in the hope that he would be touched in some way by the liturgy. She did this every Sunday for several years, and as Alzheimer's gradually made him more like a child, she worked harder to guide her husband. He would always sit peacefully in the pew, and at Communion time, she would put her arm around her husband and slowly guide him toward the Blessed Sacrament. As she did so, I couldn't help thinking about all the memories they once shared—memories that were now hers alone. As he received the Blessed Sacrament, on his face was gentle humility, innocence, and serenity—qualities that too few of us have as we receive. There is no doubt that Jesus found a joyful resting place in this man's heart, as Jesus yearns to be with the innocent. Though his mind abandoned him, His Savior never did. And his wife never did.

Love is good when it's easy. Love is great when it's hard.

Though this was one of the greatest love stories I ever witnessed, it strikes me that *every* great story is a love story, and every love story is a great story. In fiction, the glamorized stories often take place in exotic locales or on beautiful beaches. But in reality, love is often found in awkward places. The greatest love story of them all started in a manger for animals.

Although you may not realize it, you homeschooling fathers are part of a love story. You are constantly writing chapters in a book that may never make it to the silver screen, but are worth their weight in gold. It might be teaching Grammar 9 to your daughter, taking your sons to an aquarium for science class, or leaving work early to take your little daughter to the children's library. These are chapters in your book of life.

We all go through hard times in the homeschooling process. Our children may not want to do their studies, they may have a hard time grasping the academic concepts, and they may not be ready with words of thanks to their parents. When it seems that your efforts as a father are becoming a thankless job, and you're not getting the recognition you deserve, remember what Jesus endured. As Jesus watched from the Cross, few were there to comfort Him. Those who were cured of blindness were not there to see His Passion. The mutes who were cured were not there to sing His praises. The lame who were cured did not walk up Calvary with Him. Since most of the greatest acts of love are not followed by words of thanks, we cannot perform actions with the hope of thanks—we perform our actions with the hope of love. When Mother Teresa passed away, a note was found among her belongings. The note read: "The good you do today will often be forgotten. Do good anyway."

Fathers, God appreciates your work, even if no one else does.

I think in a way we fathers are like that wife in my parish. While she could look back on all the memories she had made over the years, we fathers can look forward to all the memories that we will make as the years go by. We are making memories, and we are showing our children how much we love them. Make no mistake: homeschooling is a love story. It is a love story between children and their parents, between a husband and wife, and between a family and God. Our children may need to be led by the hand to their destination, but we should be honored that it is our hand that guides them.

A Night Out

When we were married, Lisa and I made a pact to go out on a date at least once a week. And, more or less, we've been faithful to this promise. There was a time when these dates were glamorous. When we went out on dates in the first two years of marriage, we would both get dressed up, hire a babysitter for Athan and go out to dinner. We had a favorite restaurant that was about fifteen miles from our house. It was a quaint little restaurant that was tucked away that only a few people knew about. The owners served food that was so exceptional that it didn't matter what you ordered—you knew it would always taste fantastic. The conversation was as light as the pastry before us, as Lisa would tell me something funny that little Athan did during the day, or something that he had just learned to do. We'd set aside about two hours for the experience, casually working our way through appetizers, gently sipping our Cabernet Sauvignon, until the final bite of our dessert and the last sip of our coffee was finished. After dinner, on summer nights, we would open the windows to our car and smell the wafts of fresh-cut grass, and feel the warm night air as we drove over the magnificent, lush, green hills of the Shenandoah Valley to make our way back home.

As I said, we've been faithful to that weekly promise, but as time has gone by, the definition of "date" has evolved to include almost anything. What amounts to a date these days? What about a trip to the hardware store to get a new drill, and stopping for a cup of coffee on the way home? That's a date. What about a trip to drop off the boys at basketball practice and grabbing an ice cream cone? That counts.

However, one recent "date" pushed reasonable boundaries. The idea for the date was hatched when we learned that our washing machine was broken. For obvious reasons, few things strike more fear in a mother of nine than a broken washing machine. After a few days, we were forced to make a decision: wear dirty clothes, or "outsource" our laundry needs (meaning, in less thrilling terms, going to a laundromat). We opted for the latter, and as we were loading our clothes in our SUV, Lisa and I announced to the children that we were going on a date—a laundry date.

If you haven't been to a laundromat in a few years, let me fill you in. Other than bowling alleys, it would be difficult to cut yourself a slice of Americana more accurately than visiting a laundromat. Laundromats show you how people *really* are. That's not necessarily good. Most people in America spend at least a few seconds grooming before going somewhere; they don't necessarily primp, but at least they'll wear clean clothes and comb their hair. Not so with laundromats. People seem to take it as a given that they will not run into anyone they know. It's a gamble, but it's one that they seem surprisingly willing to take.

There are unstated rules of laundromats. For instance, every one I have visited in the past fifteen years has had a Ms. Pac Man machine. Ms. Pac Man machines are as common as the ubiquitous Buddha statues in nail salons. No one really knows *why* they're there, but you can expect one when you go.

There are also *stated* rules. *First*, you are not allowed to dye clothes in their washing machines. Every once in a while, you might think to yourself: "You know, I think I'd look good in brown. Why not dye all my clothes that color?" Perhaps a great idea, but don't expect to be able to do it in a laundromat. *Second*, alcohol is generally not allowed. That's a shame, because you really haven't lived until you've mixed drinks on a clothes-folding table. So leave the cocktail shaker at home. *Third*, pets are not allowed. This rule is an inconvenience to say the least. The summer after high school, I got to be friends with a girl who trained tiny Capuchin monkeys to assist people. Now you're telling people that they can't bring their monkeys to help with the folding and sorting? Who, pray tell, should do this work?

Two hours after we'd arrived, as we loaded the clothes back in the car and drove home, there were a few similarities with those early dates that only the most hardened cynic would fail to see. Instead of the smell of fresh-cut grass, we could enjoy the fragrance of fabric softener wafting through our car. Instead of wine, we drank orange Gatorade. Instead of the scenery of rolling green hills and plains, we could enjoy the understated ambiance of an unlit alley. Of course, we still had a great time. I'm guessing that many of us homeschooling fathers have "dates" likes this from time to time. The next time you do, remember my twofold piece of advice: *first*, try to remember that the "who" is more important than the "what" in many of life's activities, and *second*, take a lot of quarters.

Under the Sea... Almost

My fourteen-year-old son Demetrius has long had aspirations to be a marine biologist. And as a parent who seeks to encourage his children in their dreams, for several years, I had promised Demetrius that, one day, I would take him to a place in Florida where it is possible to snorkel.

So, on a recent family vacation to the Sunshine State, I woke Demetrius early in the morning, and announced to him that his wait was over. An hour later, on a sunny, azure skied, 80-degree day, we checked in, got our gear, and headed for the water. So far, so good.

But there was one major drawback: though Demetrius swims like a citizen of the underwater city of Atlantis, I swim like a resident of Mars. You have heard of running in place? I can *swim in place*—unintentionally, of course. Watching me in the water is probably like watching someone swim on a treadmill. I swim through water like I'm swimming through glue. Not that this is all bad. I single-handedly disprove evolutionary theory: no one who has ever seen me swim could rationally conclude that man is evolved from sea life.

Despite being aquatically challenged, I wanted to share this snorkeling experience with Demetrius, and undaunted by pride, I figured that I could solve my little problem by using a life-jacket. To my land-locked friends, let me warn you: a life-jacket is the scarlet letter of nautical life. They are awkward, bulky, and brightly colored, presumably as a way of proclaiming to the world in no uncertain terms: "I am a poor swimmer." Matters aren't helped much when you can't remember the term "life-preserver" and you ask the attendant instead where you can obtain a "floaty."

So there we were: Demetrius, snorkeling and taking pictures with his waterproof camera, looking like a consultant to a Jacques Cousteau expedition—and his dad, who resembled more of a fishing lure than a human. It occurred to me that I couldn't have looked too dignified to spectators. Even the fish must have been confused. But as I drifted along these waters, I realized something more important than how ridiculous I looked: Demetrius was having the time of his life. Watching your son do something that he has wanted to do his whole life—and doing it so well—has to make you feel good as a father, even if your choice of swimwear involves styrofoam.

As the day went on, I found myself able to be more proficient in the water, while Demetrius patiently instructed me. By the end of the day, even though I didn't learn to swim well, I did learn to snorkel effectively while holding a floating "noodle." And in truth, I had a pretty great day, too.

There might be a lesson for homeschooling parents in this. For all of the things that homeschooling *is*, it *isn't* glitzy. You don't have the school plays that your children's friends have; at best, you have puppet shows. You don't get to wear school uniforms that make the education seem "official"; your kids wear very unofficial-looking sweatpants to religion class. You don't have a science lab; the closest you've ever come to doing a chemistry experiment in your home may have involved cinnamon and French toast. At least at times, you don't have much acceptance from others—even your friends.

You often feel like you're behind, and this causes its own set of problems. If children in formal schools fall behind academically, people often wonder what's wrong with the *children*. If children taught at home fall behind academically, people often wonder what's wrong with the *parents*. When you hear other parents brag about how well their children are doing in school, you can't really do the same about your own kids. "After all," the logic goes, "if the parent does the grading, why wouldn't the children get good grades?"

Sometimes we homeschooling parents seem to float along, realizing that we need help just to keep our heads above water. We might feel like we look foolish along the way, or feel like we don't fit in. But we are *in* the water, rather than watching our children swim by as we stand on the shore.

Many educational systems claim to be based on sound principles: the look-say method, the Montessori method, and so forth. Homeschooling parents may differ in their academic nuances, but the undercurrent for our homeschooling approach is that we love our children, and, though we are human, we don't fall too short on that level. I love Demetrius, just like I love all my children. That's why I accept standing out from the crowd. That's what got me in the water. Many homeschooling methods tend to work because of this single motivating factor: the love we have for our children.

As the years have gone by, you may have felt like you have looked foolish homeschooling, but you've probably done a great job. In between administering math quizzes and watching SAT preparation videos, instead of thinking of your failures, try to take a little time to ponder what you have already accomplished. You've made a lot of sacrifices for your children—some were easy, and some were hard. But you've spent a big part of your life trying to help your children grow closer to God. I have a feeling that one day we'll compare notes on how we made it all work, and on the role that grace played in our successes. When that day comes, please look for me. I'll be the guy in the neon green floaty.

Raspberry Sorbet

It had been a rough day. I was buried in paperwork at the office, two of my children were sick, and the rain had been drizzling since morning. It would be only a slight exaggeration to say that the highlight of my day was paying the orthodontist bill. After I left work, and picked up my eleven-year-old son Tarcisius (or as he is simply nicknamed, "T") to drive him to his baseball game, there was no reason to think that this was going to be a special day.

After I parked the car, T and I walked to the dugout together, and we noticed that the sun had decided to make an appearance for the first time that day. Since we were late, T was not in the starting lineup, so I grabbed a bucket of baseballs and gave him some soft-toss pitches between innings. In the third or fourth inning, after two batters had reached base, T was put into the lineup, and he stepped into the batter's box.

Now, to visualize this story properly, it helps to understand that T has been blessed with size. When he used to play "Tee-Ball" (a game he thought was named for him), he seemed like a giant compared to the other boys. Though he had just celebrated his eleventh birthday, he stood about five feet, four inches tall. And if it's possible to be muscular at eleven years old, T was that. This is slightly ironic, and here's why. When he was a baby, we got the standard, "What a handsome baby" comments, complete with smiles, but then a funny thing happened. People would ask his name, and Lisa and I told them: "Tarcisius." The smiles would leave people's faces, they would give their heads a quarter turn, don a look of disbelief, and then inform us: "You know, people are going to make fun of him with that name. They're going to call him 'Sissy.'" I think that T's size is God's little joke to would-be name callers.

As T stepped into the batter's box, he tapped the plate with his bat, dug in his cleats, and waited for the pitch. A few seconds later, as the centerfielder looked up and saw the baseball going over his head, he raced back to the wall and grabbed it on the warning track. When the ball finally returned to the infield, T was standing on second base, looking over at his teammates and smiling.

This entire process took about twelve seconds, and yet for that moment in time, to me, all was right with the world. This wasn't the first time T got a hit, and it wasn't even the first time that T hit a 2-RBI double. But in baseball, these moments are always special. Though I had undergone a difficult day up to that point, this game was just another reminder of something to a lover of the game: baseball has a therapeutic value.

At some fine restaurants (I am told) diners are sometimes offered raspberry sorbet between meal courses. It removes some of the conflicting memory of what has gone before and prepares the palate for what lies ahead.

It strikes me that baseball is raspberry sorbet for the mind.

I've never been comfortable comparing baseball to any other sport. In my mind, it's not fair to the other sports. It's not that football or soccer don't require intense training or athleticism. It's just that baseball transcends its genre.

Baseball lovers quickly grow tired of explaining to others why the game is beautiful. Like all art forms, it tends to transcend literary description. But to the skeptics, consider the following points that many baseball writers have often observed over the years. At the highest level of the game, not only is a typical ball thrown at a velocity of over ninety miles per hour, but the pitcher is trying to do everything he can to make the ball take an erratic flight in the air. A ninety-five mile per hour pitch would be difficult enough to handle without it changing direction just as the batter is trying to hit it. The batter, concentrating on a white ball that is less than three inches in diameter, must decide whether to hit that ball in about one-fifth of a second with a bat that is only about two and one-half inches thick. Not only must he hit the ball, but he should hit the *center* of the ball. Not only does he have to hit the ball with the bat, but he must hit the ball with the *sweet spot* of the bat, which is about three inches in size.

With all the things going through his mind, there are thoughts that he must *not* ponder. The hitter must try not to think about the fact that the baseball might hit him in the head and end his career. He must block out the noise of tens of thousands of fans—many of whom desperately want to see him fail, and are not shy about telling him their feelings. He must also disregard the fact that if he does not do well enough, he and his family might suffer financially. Twenty years of practice will be for naught if he fails enough times. But if the batter hits the ball well, a five-ounce ball can travel more than 400 feet. When you consider what is involved, it is almost ridiculous to expect players to hit home runs, and yet they do. The level of dedication it takes to be great should inspire us.

It's not just the game itself that is magnificent—it is what the game can do for players. Someone once observed that "the baseball diamond defines who we are," meaning that the way we behave on a baseball field tells us a lot about ourselves—some good and some bad. The game magnifies the player's virtues and vices, and allows him to work on both. Anyone who has played the game knows this all too well. Baseball teaches players how to deal with failure because there's a lot of it, even for great players. Sometimes strikeouts are remembered more than hits. Otherwise-successful careers can even be defined by failures. Defensive errors are not just criticized, but are put on a massive scoreboard. No other major sport does this.

Perfection is expected.

And even after having their mistakes discussed by thousands, if not millions, of people, baseball players must persevere. They must develop a positive attitude despite all the negativity. They must not only learn to deal with adversity—they must learn to *thrive* on adversity. Maybe the best example of this was Babe Ruth's affirmation: "Every strikeout gets me closer to my next home run." Good baseball players *define* perseverance.

In order to improve, a player must have the humility to admit even slight imperfections, and then correct them. He must seek the help of others to improve: batting coaches, managers, and fellow players. In other walks of life, once a certain level of greatness has been achieved, people often slouch into a life of contentment. Baseball players don't. They can't because there is always someone ready to take their place.

When I coached baseball at Christendom College, I used to tell my players that baseball didn't grant them the luxury of harping on past mistakes. The motto for our team, which became a motto for myself and my family, was: "Remember your mistakes long enough to learn from them—and then forget them." What better analogy is there to living the Catholic Faith?

You may train very hard for something—a chance—only to fail. But baseball teaches another valuable lesson—that failure is transitory. Baseball teaches you that you can be down two strikes, but you're not out. You could have struck out three times one night, but redemption lies in your fourth time at bat, and that may be the one that makes all the difference.

Baseball has many lessons to teach, and you don't need to make it to the major leagues to discover them. Perhaps at its highest level of achievement, it is a game played between fathers and sons. Though we live in an age of "soccer moms," I miss a time and place when there were "baseball dads." I think most of us would love to go back in time and play catch with our own dads. While we can't do that, we do have the opportunity to make a memory today with our own children. As homeschooling fathers, a lot of our time with our children is devoted to math lessons, spelling quizzes, and book reports. Let's find some time to discover the fun part of learning—to learn about the game of baseball together, and get to know your sons (and daughters) in the process.

As Tarcisius and I walked back to the car, I think we realized that we had taught each other a lesson. He showed me how great it was to be eleven years old again, and I showed him how great it was to be the father of a special (and not so) little boy.

Conversations with Children

Hoping to eat some breakfast before I dealt with the ravages of the financial markets, I woke up early one morning before the rest of the family and started making myself breakfast. Maybe roused from the smell of coffee, five-year-old Dominica wandered downstairs in her slippers and Dora the Explorer Christmas pajamas, and observed me cooking. Perhaps expecting something more in the way of Apple Cinnamon Cheerios, she looked at me cracking eggs, and asked me what I was making. I told her I was making an "egg white omelet."

She had never heard of such a thing, so she asked me what that was. So I told her, "It's an omelet that uses only the white part of the egg."

Dominica paused for a moment, quizzically pondered this idea in her head, then scrunched her nose, looked up at me and asked: "You mean, you're only going to eat the *shell*?"

It's one of those moments as a homeschooling father that you realize that it's your child's *interpretation* of life that keeps things interesting.

Last fall, I spent about forty or fifty hours assembling my oldest three children's homeschool lesson plans. I was really proud of how it all turned out. I had assembled copies of original source readings, made sure they had access to the proper classical pieces for their music lessons, and so forth. I really spent a lot of time on the lesson plans, but in the weeks to come, I became over-reliant on the fact that I had done the initial lesson plan work. I quickly realized that homeschooling does not simply consist of putting together some lesson plans and having the children do the assignments. It consists of analyzing their *interpretations* of what they are learning. A remembrance from my past illustrates this point.

When I attended Christendom College, I asked one of the professors how he endured reading thirty term papers written on the same topic. He answered that all the papers interested him, not necessarily based on the topic, but how the student *interpreted* the topic. He said: "I'm not reading the *Odyssey* papers with the hope that the student will uncover some new aspect of Homer. Instead, I want to know what John Clark thinks about the *Odyssey*." Frankly, I was flattered that he *cared* what I thought about it.

That brief conversation provides an academic backdrop of the father's role in homeschooling.

When I observed Athan reading Homer's *Odyssey*, I understood what the teacher meant. The access to literature or theology or economics provides an insight into the student himself, and it's a *fascinating* insight. I want to know what my children think about the *Odyssey*. I want to know what interests *them*.

What we need to do as fathers is to talk to our children about what they are learning, and what *they* think about it. This process doesn't have to be very formal. That's one of the great things about homeschooling—the lack of formality. I can have serious, intellectual discussions about economics or theology or science with my children while I'm wearing Pillsbury Doughboy pajamas. (Once I step out the door, it's hard to be taken seriously with that fashion risk.)

If you do want to make it more formal, do this: take your children out to a meal once a week. Go out for a pancake breakfast with your son or daughter before work one day, and ask about the subjects he or she is studying. Take your oldest children to dinner and have them bring their history books. Strike up a conversation about history. Ask them what they thought about the historical decisions of leaders. "Do you think that George Washington made a good decision?" "What do you think that St. Augustine was trying to teach us by writing his *Confessions*?"

I ask my children questions like this all the time: "What's your favorite saint book this year?" "Why do you think Mark Twain wrote that?" "Based on the book, what can you guess about the background of the author?" "What problems are you having with math?" "What new piece are you learning to play on violin?" "Were you scared/excited/surprised when you shot that free throw/fielded that ground ball/caught that pass?"

You might surprise your children if you ask them questions like this. Your children observe you going to work every day and doing something, in their eyes, mysterious and pretty important. By conversing with them about academics, you're showing them that what *they're* doing is pretty important, too.

As my children get older, I have to admit: I'm learning a lot from them. Last week, my oldest son taught me something about the *Summa*. My daughter taught me something about St. Catherine Labouré. The other day, one of my children told me why the sky was blue. Maybe I shouldn't admit this, but I never really knew why. I was the child who apparently never asked. As a father, it's very rewarding to learn their viewpoints.

I'm even learning from Dominica, who, on the literary side, is an expert on Dr. Seuss, and prides herself on her encyclopedic knowledge of zoo animals.

I just might have her wait a little while on the cooking.

Plum Pudding and Scrabble

My children and I were recently speaking about when and how I began homeschooling as a child. The textbook answer is that I went to a day school called Mater Dei Academy in Columbus, Ohio, for five years and started homeschooling in the sixth grade. But in its truest sense, homeschooling begins long before a workbook or a #3 pencil box is ever opened. And the more I considered the idea of when it all began, the more my memories turned toward two special women who helped shape me.

If you are truly blessed, you will have one grandmother in your life who makes such an impact on your childhood that her influence stays with you forever.

I had two.

Born and raised in Scotland, Jean Clark, my paternal grandmother, had a gift for "grandmothering." I have always enjoyed cooking, and my grandmother may have been my biggest influence. To this day, I have not met her culinary equal. She could look into a nearly empty refrigerator (or as she called it, an "icebox") and produce some of the greatest tasting food I've ever eaten. That's an accomplishment, made even greater when you consider that, as the saying goes, most Scottish cuisine is based on a dare. She also knew how to make dozens of types of cookies from scratch, which she gladly baked for us. Every year around Christmas, she baked plum pudding with coins in it. My brothers and I would excitedly search our pieces to see who had the most valuable slice. (I'm assuming that this is a Scottish tradition, which makes me wonder how many Scotsmen are walking around with quarters in their stomachs.)

Whenever she babysat me, which was often, we would play games, like "Go Fish," or she would take me for a walk down to the lake by her apartment to feed the resident ducks. We also loved to watch *The Price is Right* together. I probably learned more about the price of things watching this show than any other single factor in my youth. I also learned to bid properly for items, and to avoid overbidding, which may have had a profound influence on my career choice.

She also had a deep love for Scripture. Born and raised a Protestant, she would spend hours a day reading her Bible. It was impossible to know her but miss the fact that she loved her Bible. That makes an impact.

She was stricken with arthritis for much of her life, and in her last few years, she needed help walking. I used to help her walk up the staircase to her bedroom every night, just to make sure she wouldn't fall. When I got there, she would often hand me a dollar bill for my trouble. "You don't have to pay me, Grammie," I'd tell her.

"I know, but I want to," she'd tell me. She cared for me when I was little—now I could care for her. This is a beautiful part of family life—the caregiver and the one who is cared for switch roles—and a sadly absent one from much of American life.

Though she lived until she was eighty-nine years old and I was nineteen, I don't remember her ever saying a mean word to—or about—anyone. The closest I ever heard her come to it was just before the royal wedding of Charles and Diana, she commented that Lady Diana was "plain." "But," she explained, "plain is beautiful." I felt sad lately as I watched some of the royal wedding of Prince William and Lady Kate, because my grandmother wasn't able to see it. But maybe in the Providence of God, she was.

When I was about nine years old, my friends came over and listened to a conversation I had with my grandmother. After I left the room and walked over to them, they asked me a question that shocked me: "How do you understand what your grandmother is saying?" Until that point, I never realized she had a thick Scottish accent—that was just the way Grammie talked. Twenty years later, whenever I speak to someone from Scotland, I think about how much I still miss her, and always will.

St. Teresa of Avila famously prayed, "May God protect me from gloomy saints," meaning that if one has the faith and a true love of God, there is cause for great joy. Jacqueline Lynch, my maternal grandmother, was the opposite of gloomy. In fact, I have never met a truly happier person. Someone should have told my grandmother that she was no longer seventeen years old, but no one ever had the heart to tell her; if they had, she wouldn't have taken it seriously anyway.

I have never met someone who simultaneously shared a deep joy of games and a profound reverence for the Mass more than she did. She was never too busy to play Monopoly or Scrabble with us, and never too busy to talk about the Catholic Faith with us. She often treated us children like we were more important than adults.

When my brothers and I visited her over one summer vacation, we would get up early in the morning and sit in the living room talking to each other, playing games, or watching TV. When she entered the room, she would walk over to each of us, give us a big hug as if she hadn't seen us in years, smile, and tell each of us how glad she was that we were with her. We stayed for a three-week vacation, but she did that routine every single morning of our visit. Perhaps aside from my little children, I have never known someone as glad to see me as my grandmother.

One afternoon when I was about ten years old, I was playing with my cousin's Western toy gun set. Someone mentioned to me that I shouldn't be playing with it because it wasn't mine, so I carefully put the toy down. The next day, my grandmother came home from shopping and handed me a Western toy gun and holster of my own. She explained that she had bought the toy for me because I was so careful with my cousin's toy, and had put it back as soon as I thought about the fact that it wasn't mine. No one should wonder why today I am such an ardent defender of property rights.

Charles Dickens wrote that after Scrooge's conversion, no one kept the spirit of Christmas better. I knew someone who did. My grandmother started shopping for the *next* Christmas in late December. Though she had dozens of grandchildren, when we all visited on Christmas Day, she had gifts laid out for every single one of us with our names by them. Three years before she died, she announced that she had cancer. Possibly thinking that it might take her that year, she put up a Christmas tree, perhaps hoping that she would make it until Christmas. She *did* survive through that Christmas, but she never wanted to take down the tree. As long as that tree was there, she would make it. That little Christmas tree lasted for three more years, and so did she.

I was recently having some difficulty with a project at work and, like all good Catholic men of faith, I tried to think of the right prayer to say, and for that matter, which saint to ask for intercession. The idea of my grandmother came to me, so I quietly offered a prayer to her, and in the grandson-to-grandmother vernacular, I whispered simply: "Grammie, I need you to bail me out." Needless to say, my prayer was answered, and in a way that seemed to communicate to me: "I've never stopped thinking about you—I'll always be your grandmother."

It's hard to draw the line between where homeschooling begins and ends. We homeschooling parents are constantly looking for a better textbook or for better flash cards or for better software to teach our children. These are all important things that we need to do as homeschooling parents. But as we're trying to help our children grow into faithful Catholics, let's not overlook an obvious clue—that many of the people in our lives and the lives of our children are able to help us in a way that mere books cannot. May our Lord bless all those who have had a beneficial influence on our children's lives, and may God bless all the grandmothers.

Afterword: Questions, Answers, and Errors

Occasionally, when people ask me about my columns, they wonder if I'm making this stuff up. So I thought I would take a few moments and answer the more frequent questions. Here they are.

Are those the real names of your children? Yes. Unlike in *Dragnet*, the names have not been changed to protect the innocent. Along with middle names and ages (as this book goes to print), they are: Athanasius Chrysostom (18), Veronica Marie (16), Demetrius Innocent (14), Tarcisius Bellarmine (12), Philomena Guadalupe (10), Dominica Rose (8), Bonaventure Duns Scotus (6), Immaculata Faustyna (4), and Mary Katherine (2).

Oddly enough, when I recite these names to people, the one that throws them for a loop is Mary Katherine. After all the other names, normalcy seems out of place. I love that. Lisa and I also thought that the first Mary Kay Clark was so successful that the world needed another.

By the way, I am open to suggestions for the next child, if by the generosity of God there is a tenth. Maybe Lisa and I should initiate a naming contest—submit ideas for the name and the winner gets a free dinner for four at Jack in the Box. If you are inclined to do so, be sure that the name is: 1) at least four syllables, 2) the name of a doctor of the Church, and/or 3) someone who directly conversed with Jesus.

Do you mind surrendering some of your privacy for the column? I guess people think I'm being too open with my life when I mention things like our "Bowling for

Bedtimes" contests. However, since when did privacy become a Catholic virtue anyway? It's not listed in the *Summa*, but if it were, St. Thomas would probably have had a section called "Vices Opposed to Privacy," in which he would have listed "child-rearing" as the primary vice. Listen, anyone who has nine children couldn't possibly have privacy as a top priority. At any given time, my bedroom door has no working lock on it. As a matter of fact, it may not even have a working doorknob at the moment. There are downsides to this, not the least of which is that over the years, the children have snuck into our room during the night and proceeded to wet the bed.

You're asking about *privacy*? I'll settle for a dry place to sleep.

Are you having any more children? This question logically follows the one about privacy. When I am asked this question, I think about growing up in a family of seven boys. When I was growing up, people used to ask me about my family, and I loved to shock them by telling them I had *six* brothers. They would almost always follow up by commenting: "Your mom must be a saint!" Then I would joke to them: "She would have had more, but she wanted a career, too." (Catholics don't get this joke. They think I'm serious.) I'm sure my mom and dad wanted to have more children, and I've always had a touch of sadness that my mom never had a daughter. A sister among us may also have balanced out some of the more testosterone-laden things that my brothers and I did growing up, like shooting arrows at the house, making our own ammunition, having *Space Invaders* contests on the Atari game system, ghost-riding bicycles down our street, fighting with colored pencils, making fishing lures out of Coca-Cola cans, or dressing up in Ninja outfits and hurling throwing-stars in our garage—basically the things that happen when there is a lack of female influence. One of the most emasculating things that any of us did growing up was polishing the gun cabinet. (Oddly enough—and it seems even odder in retrospect—we were pretty good at homeschooling.) Although we boys may have resisted the idea at first, a sister would have been a welcome addition to our family.

Realistically, I doubt that anyone who has nine children suddenly decides that they can't have ten. Our philosophy is that there is always room for one more at the table—even if it's a card table.

How do you do it all? Well, I'm not sure what "all" is, but I'm pretty sure I'm not doing it "all." Happily, I am doing *some* of it. For instance, Veronica once had a history test and she was having a hard time remembering the important facts in the life of Josef Stalin. If I were doing it "all," I would have quizzed her over and over until she remembered the communist's life in great detail. However, that is a little depressing. So I set the facts to one of her favorite songs. Unbelievably, she remembered the rather esoteric lyrics days later. That is doing "some" of it.

I suspect that most fathers are doing "some of it" too. Keep at it.

Works Cited

p. 6
Chambers, Whittaker. *Witness*. New York: Random House, 1952.

p. 10
The National Fatherhood Initiative web site, http://www.fatherhood.org/media/consequences-of-father-absence-statistics (accessed October 12, 2011).

p. 12
Wallerstein, Judith, Julia Lewis, and Sandra Blakeslee. *The Unexpected Legacy of Divorce: A 25 Year Landmark Study*. New York: Hyperion, 2000.

p. 13
Ratzinger, Joseph (Pope Benedict XVI). Translated by Adrian J. Walker. *Jesus of Nazareth*. New York: Doubleday. 2007.

p. 14
Simon, George Thomas. *Glenn Miller and His Orchestra*. New York: Thomas Y. Crowell Publishers, 1974.

p. 19, 20, 24
Kowalska, Sister M. Faustina. *Divine Mercy in My Soul*. Stockbridge, MA: Marian Press, 1987.

p. 27
Pope Pius XI. "Ad Catholici Sacerdotii." 1935. The Vatican Official Website. http://www.vatican.va/holy_father/pius_xi/encyclicals/documents/hf_p-xi_enc_19351220_ad-catholici-sacerdotii_en.html (accessed October 6, 2011).

p. 28
Bowden, John Edward, editor. *The Spirit of the Cure of Ars*. Translated from the French by M. L'Abbe Monnin. London: Burns, Lambert, and Oates, 1865. Page 72.

p. 29, 37
The Pieta Prayer Book. Hickory Corners, MI: MLOR Corporation, 2004.

p. 31
St. Louis Marie-Grignion de Montfort. *True Devotion to Mary*. Rockford, IL: Tan Books and Publishers, 1985.

Pope Leo XIII. "Supremi Apostolatus Officio." 1883. The Vatican Official Website. http://www.vatican.va/holy_father/leo_xiii/encyclicals/documents/hf_l-xiii_enc_01091883_supremi-apostolatus-officio_en.html (accessed October 6, 2011).

Power-Waters, Alma. *St. Catherine Laboure and the Miraculous Medal.* San Francisco: Ignatius Press, 1990.

p. 32

Pope John Paul II, "Rosarium Virginis Mariae," 2002. The Vatican Official Website. http://www.vatican.va/holy_father/john_paul_ii/apost_letters/documents/hf_jp-ii_apl_20021016_rosarium-virginis-mariae_en.html (Emphasis in original.) (accessed October 11, 2011).

Pope Pius XI, "Ingravescentibus Malis," 1937. http://www.vatican.va/holy_father/pius_xi/encyclicals/documents/hf_p-xi_enc_29091937_ingravescentibus-malis_en.html (accessed October 11, 2011).

p. 34

Pope Leo XIII, "Quamquam Pluries," 1889. The Vatican Official Website. http://www.vatican.va/holy_father/leo_xiii/encyclicals/documents/hf_l-xiii_enc_15081889_quamquam-pluries_en.html (accessed October 11, 2011).

p. 54

Pope Pius XI, "Casti Connubii," 1930. The Vatican Official Website. http://www.vatican.va/holy_father/pius_xi/encyclicals/documents/hf_p-xi_enc_31121930_casti-connubii_en.html (accessed October 11, 2011).

p. 89

"Perseverance." Def. 1 & 2. *The Random House Dictionary of the English Language*, second edition. 1987.

p. 98

Minow, Newton and Craig L. LaMay. *Abandoned in the Wasteland: Children, Television, and the First Amendment.* New York: Hill and Wang, 1996.

p. 114

Thompson, Francis. Wilfred Meynell, Editor. *Three Volumes in One, Volume One: Poems.* Westminster, MD: The Newman Bookshop, 1947.